# OLYMPIC GAMES
# IN ANCIENT GREECE

# OLYMPIC GAMES
# IN ANCIENT GREECE

## by Shirley Glubok
## and Alfred Tamarin

HARPER & ROW, PUBLISHERS

Title page illustration:

*Athlete wearing victor's fillet. Roman copy of statue by Polyclitus, fifth century* B.C.

The Metropolitan Museum of Art, Fletcher Fund, 1925

map by Dyno Lowenstein

Library of Congress Cataloging in Publication Data
Glubok, Shirley.
  Olympic Games in ancient Greece.

  SUMMARY: An account of the Olympic games as they probably occurred at the height of their classic glory.
  1. Olympic games (Ancient)—Juvenile literature.
[1. Olympic games (Ancient)] I. Tamarin, Alfred, joint author. II. Title.
GV23.G55 1976        796.4'8        75-25408
ISBN 0-06-022047-3
ISBN 0-06-022048-1 lib. bdg.

# OLYMPIC GAMES
# IN ANCIENT GREECE

# CONTENTS

# PRELIMINARIES

HOW THRILLING IT would be to open this story of the Olympic Games in ancient Greece with the sound of a trumpet recalling the signal which proclaimed the beginning of the Olympiads for more than a thousand years. But since it is not possible, we have to start with less musical, but equally exciting, material —pictures painted on vases, words scratched on the bases of statues, poetic odes, accounts from ancient histories, dialogues spoken by actors in Greek dramas, and casual references to lost lists of Olympic victors in the works of later authors.

Our account of the ancient Games takes the form of an ideal Olympiad set around the year 400 B.C.—a year that is both early and late in the long span of Greek history. This year can be considered late when compared to 776 B.C., the date that marks the start of the Olympic Games and the beginning of recorded history in Greece. Athletic competitions in ancient Greece were even older than the written record. In the epic story of the *Iliad*, written in the eighth century B.C., the Greek poet Homer described funeral games that were really sporting events. They were held, he said, outside the walls of besieged

*Entrance to the stadium at Olympia, seen from the* altis.
photo by N.A. Tombazi

9

Troy five hundred years before. And the *Odyssey* contains a description of a boxing match.

We chose the fifth century B.C. because the Olympic Games had by then reached the height of their classic glory. Olympia had become a major focus for the Greek world, which congregated in the sacred grove every fourth year to cheer on a favorite champion, as well as to exchange the latest news and gossip. By 400 B.C. the shrine at Olympia shone with splendid works of architecture and art. The Greek city-states vied with one another to erect treasury houses to glorify their names, and filled them with magnificent offerings to the gods worshiped at Olympia. The Temple of Zeus was finally completed, and in it was the masterpiece of the sculptor Phidias: the towering gold-and-ivory statue of Zeus with his head almost touching the ceiling.

Despite setting our ideal Games in the century of Olympia's greatest glory, we still find it necessary occasionally to take steps forward and backward in time. For instance, several events are described that actually were added later, such as the contest for heralds and trumpeters, which did not start until a few years after 400 B.C. A list of important dates at the back of this book will help the reader keep track of the changes which took place in the Olympic Games and in Greek history.

To appreciate the ancient Olympic Games, some of the generally accepted standards of modern athletic competition have to be re-examined and seen in a completely different light. In ancient games the style and grace of the competitor were regarded highly, but winning first place was all that mattered.

In ancient times there were no stopwatches to register the time of a race. No measurements were recorded of the length of a jump or of a javelin or discus throw. Team games were unknown. And even though Greece has thousands of miles of coast line and hundreds of offshore islands, no water sports were included in the program of events.

For the first two hundred years of Olympic history, no systematic record was kept of the events and the victors. Now and then a statue with the name of an Olympic champion chiseled on the base has been found, often shattered beyond repair, leaving only half a name or less to posterity. Using every source available, the writer Hippias of Elis finally compiled a list of Olympic victors at the end of the fifth century B.C. A century later the Greek philosopher Aristotle revised the first list, but neither the original version nor the revision survived. The existence of these early lists is known only through references in the works of even later authors. At other times the names of Olympic winners turned up on scraps of paper or parchment, or sometimes on the backs of other documents which survived in bits and pieces. One list was put together by the Roman chronicler Sextus Julius Africanus. The most valuable information about Olympia was recorded by the Roman traveler and geographer Pausanias, who visited the site in the second century A.D.

Important sources of pictorial information about Greek athletics are magnificent vases decorated with scenes of the sports that were played at athletic festivals, including the one at Olympia. Some of these vases were cups and bowls; others were amphora that were filled with olive oil and awarded as prizes to victors in the Pan-Athenaic Games, which were held in Athens and celebrated the birthday of the city's patron goddess, Athena.

The most important of the Pan-Hellenic (all-Greek) Games in ancient times were held at Olympia at regular four-year intervals to honor Zeus, the king of the gods. Other festivals were staged in other parts of Greece during the intervening years. At Delphi, high up on the southern slope of Mount

Parnassus, was the stadium for the Pythian Games celebrating Apollo. At Nemea, other games honored Zeus, while competitions at Isthmia were held for Poseidon, god of the sea. In addition to the Pan-Hellenic Games, there were countless other local festivals, probably in every community of any size. Out of these contests emerged the champions whose names have been immortalized by victories at Olympia, Delphi, Nemea, and Isthmia.

Writing an account of the ancient Olympic Festival involved chronicling the history of Greece, though only in the sketchiest of ways. Reflected in the Olympic Games are the rise and fall of the Greek city-state (*polis*); the founding of the Greek colonies in Asia, Africa, and Europe; the bitter civil wars between the city-states; the threat of invasion by the Persians; and finally the downfall of Greece and the ascendancy of Rome. But compiling a history of the Olympic Games as they reflect even the briefest view of the changing fortunes of the Greeks proved a complicated task. The ancient authorities did not always agree, and many modern scholars hold differing points of view also. The books by E. Norman Gardiner, *Greek Athletic Sports and Festivals*, *Olympia: Its History and Remains*, and *Athletics of the Ancient World*, are mines of information.

Often, however, writers who were not themselves athletes took literally the evidence offered by ancient vase paintings or by marble or bronze statuary. The late English classicist H.A. Harris, in his studies *Greek Athletics and Athletes* and *Sport in Greece and Rome*, took a different course and asked athletic champions to try to assume the positions illustrated by the ancient sculptors and vase painters. Many times it proved impossible for the modern athletes to run or jump in the positions depicted. The artists had sacrificed literal accuracy for pleasing designs. Getting a historical perspective on the ancient Games was made easier with the help of the late Cambridge University professor J. B. Bury. His book *A History of Greece*, first published in 1900, is now in its fourth edition (1975), co-authored by Russell Meiggs.

Certain works in German and Italian also proved helpful, particularly Luigi Moretti's complete list of Olympic winners from the first to the 293rd Olympiad, even though a few authorities disagree with some of his findings. Ludwig Drees' book, *Olympia: Gods, Artists and Athletics*, was interesting for its illustrations and for the author's theories about the religious and agricultural backgrounds of the Games. And particularly valuable was *The Olympic Games: The First Thousand Years* by M. I. Finley and H. W. Pleket (Viking, 1976).

On the question of spelling, we wanted to be consistent. When there was a choice to be made, we decided to use Latin rather than Greek spellings, except in the case of technical athletic terms. For those, we have used the Greek spellings and italicized them.

We wish to thank the following scholars who were encouraging and offered us helpful advice: George E. Mylonas, Member of the Academy of Athens, Rosa May Distinguished Professor Emeritus in the Humanities, Washington University, Honorary Professor Emeritus at the University of Athens, President Emeritus of the Archaeological Institute of America; Nikolaos Yalouris, Director, National Archaeological Museum, Athens; and, with the American School of Classical Studies at Athens: James R. McCredie, Director; Oscar Broneer, Professor Emeritus of Archaeology and Director of Excavations at Isthmia; Charles K. Williams II, field director, Ancient Corinth; and Nancy Winter, librarian.

At the German Archaeological Institute in Athens, we owe thanks to Rainer Felsch, Bernard Schmaltz, and Gerhard Schmidt. We are also grateful to Alfred Frazer, Chairman of

13

the Department of Art History and Archaeology, Columbia University, New York; to Robert Bianchi, Assistant Curator, Department of Egyptian and Classical Art, Brooklyn Museum; and to Stephanie Bianchi of Rutgers Preparatory School for her translations of all quotations from original Greek sources.

Our special thanks go to Judith Peller Hallett, Assistant Professor of Classical Studies, Boston University, for her interest and friendship and for giving us the benefit of her valuable advice.

The story of the ancient Olympic Games can provide all the excitement of a modern athletic event. In addition, it brings to life the ideal of ancient Greek youth throughout Greek history—the olive crown of victory which linked a human being to the immortals.

*The stade race. Black-figured, Pan-Athenaic prize amphora, sixth century B.C.*

The Metropolitan Museum of Art, Rogers Fund, 1914

# THE FIRST DAY:
## *The Olympiad Begins*

FOR TWO DAYS the procession had been moving slowly down the sacred way toward Olympia. At the head of the parade were the stern Hellanodicae, the purple-robed judges who would preside over the ancient Olympic Games. They were followed by other officials: referees, umpires, heralds, and trumpeters. Then came the athletes and their trainers, representing most of the city-states throughout the ancient Greek world. There were slim-waisted, long-legged runners; broad-shouldered pentathletes, who would compete in five events; and heavy-chested, large-limbed wrestlers and boxers. In the rear were sleek racehorses and their riders, and colorful chariots drawn by spirited steeds.

The sacred way to Olympia started in Elis, the city-state 34 miles away. The route skirted the low mountains of the western Peloponnesus and followed the curves along the coast line of the Ionian Sea. As the procession reached the fountain of Piera, which marked the boundary between Elis and the holy precinct of Olympia, the summer sun was sinking slowly behind the western edge of the sea. A halt was called and the marchers paused for the final rites of purification before setting foot on the sacred soil of Olympia. A pig was sacrificed and cleansing ceremonies were performed with the waters of the fountain. Then the marchers settled down among the olive trees to spend the night. The middle of the month, the time of the full moon, was just three nights away.

At the same time, travelers from all over the ancient Greek world were flocking to the Olympic Games. Some were coming on foot along the coastal road from Athens and Corinth. Others, on horseback and in carriages, crowded the valleys and jammed every road and mountain pass on the Peloponnesian peninsula. Up the Alpheus River came barges on their way from the sea about 10 miles to the west. The vessels carried Greek statesmen and merchant princes, each trying to outshine the other in magnificence. They had traveled all the way from Italy and Sicily, Marseilles, the Black Sea, and even from the northern coast of Africa. In all of these places the Greeks had established colonies, and their inhabitants still spoke only Greek and followed faithfully their homeland's customs.

Among the arriving visitors were poets and philosophers, princes and politicians, historians, soldiers, sculptors, and horse breeders. Peasants from Elis and nearby Pisa mingled with fishermen from the coast and offshore islands. With the crowds came herdsmen driving cattle to be sacrificed on the altars, merchants laden down with skins of wine, and fruit vendors. Bundles of lucky charms were being carted in for sale, as well as fillets, or headbands of wool, religious offerings, and wreaths resembling the crown of olives to be awarded each winning Olympic champion. With the peddlers came singers and dancers, gamblers and thieves, bands of clowns, acrobats, and tumblers.

Early the next morning the official procession entered Olympia and the Festival was under way. The athletes, with their trainers, families, and friends, had been in Elis for a month. For thirty days the athletes had been training under the supervision of the Hellanodicae, who were very strict. Any

16

*Men weighing merchandise. Black-figured amphora, sixth century B.C.*

The Metropolitan Museum of Art,
Joseph Pulitzer Bequest, 1947

athlete who broke a rule could expect a beating. The contestants, who had to be free Greek sons of free Greek parents, were tested and trained rigorously, and only the best were permitted to compete at Olympia. According to Philostratus (*Life of Apollonius*), before the chosen athletes had set out on the two-day march to the Games, they had been told by the judges:

> If you have practiced hard for Olympia, and if you have not been lazy, or done anything dishonorable, then go forward with confidence. But if any of you have not trained yourselves this way, then leave us and go where you choose.

At Olympia the athletes had to go through one final ceremony to reaffirm their eligibility to compete. They stood before a towering statue of Zeus, represented as the god of oaths brandishing a thunderbolt in each hand. The figure was awe-inspiring, a grim warning to anyone who might have been tempted to testify falsely. The athletes, their fathers, brothers, and trainers raised their hands over the entrails of a sacrificed pig and swore a solemn oath. They vowed that they had observed all the rules of training for at least ten months and that they would use no unfair means in order to win at the Games.

After the athletes had finished giving their oath, the judges swore to take no bribes, to make their decisions fairly, and to keep secret the reasons for their judgments. Then the final list of entries was drawn up, and the order of the preliminary heats written out on a white board. The athletes and their trainers crowded around the board, anxious to see who their opponents would be in the first matches.

The competition for heralds and trumpeters took place that same morning. Trumpeters and heralds were important officials in the Olympic Games. The trumpeter's blast signaled the start of a race, and often the notes of the horn encouraged the competitors during the final lap. Heralds proclaimed the names of the contestants, their fathers, and the communities which they represented. They also announced the winners of each Olympic event.

One trumpeter, named Herodorus, from the community of Megara, was noted for his unusual lung power, which enabled him to blow two trumpets at the same time. Herodorus won the trumpeters' competition in ten successive Olympiads.

The rest of the day was taken up with additional vows and sacrifices by the athletes and their trainers. Some made offerings to the patron gods and heroes of their own communities. Some searched out seers and soothsayers, hoping for assurances that they would be successful in the competitions. Those who did not look for supernatural help spent their time in last-minute practice.

Everywhere the athletes went, the crowds followed, excited, cheering, enthusiastic.

Overhead in the clear blue sky the sun grew intense and hot. Bright light flooded the entire terrace—called the *altis*, the Greek word meaning a grove of trees. On one side rose the Hill of Cronus, named for the father of the ancient Greek gods. The other three sides were bordered by the Alpheus and Cladeus Rivers, which joined just below the grove and emptied into the Ionian Sea, 10 miles to the west. The *altis* was a flat plain lying among gentle hills. Rain, which fell all year, kept the country green and the rivers ever-flowing. In the sunlight yellow flowers glowed amid the olive trees. Despite the excited hubbub of the crowds, a hush hung over the countryside, befitting a home of the gods.

At the foot of the Hill of Cronus was the stadium, the running track for the foot, or stade, races. According to one

*The ancient stadium at Olympia, seen from the finish line.*

photo German Archaeological Institute, Athens

Greek legend, its length had been paced out by the hero Hercules, who had set one foot in front of the other 600 times to establish a course for himself and his brothers. Another legend tells that the length of the stadium had been set at 600 feet because that was the distance Hercules could run on one lungful of air.

A ledge along one side served as a vantage point for half the spectators, while an embankment on the other side of the stadium provided a view for the remainder. When the day of the races dawned, there would be as many as 40,000 people cheering on their favorites. Beyond the embankment, toward the Alpheus River, was the Hippodrome, the course for the chariot and horse races.

There was a sense of peace about the Olympic site. It was

20

late summer; the early grain harvests had already been gathered, but the grapes were still ripening on the vines and the olives on the trees. It was a good time for the men and youths who worked in the fields and orchards to put down their tools for a while. In years past, the lull after the early harvest had often been filled with the clash of battles between neighboring city-states, but for the Olympic Games a sacred truce was declared for a period of three months.

During this time of truce all arms were forbidden at Olympia, and safe passage was guaranteed to all competitors and visitors. Yet, old rivalries were not easily forgotten, and the crowds, even as they wandered around after the athletes from their own communities, continued to eye visitors from rival city-states cautiously. The truce was originally intended to end the fighting on the Peloponnesus between the two rival city-states Elis and Pisa. But as the Greek world spread into Asia, Africa, and Europe, it became necessary to expand the area protected by the truce. Originally the truce lasted for only one month. Then it had to be extended for an additional month, then still another, to permit the competitors and spectators time to reach the banks of the Alpheus and return home.

Several months before the Olympic Games were scheduled to begin, three sacred truce bearers of Zeus left Elis and headed east and west to every city-state on the Greek mainland and every Greek community overseas. These heralds were welcomed throughout the states of the Greek-speaking world. With official ceremony, the heralds proclaimed the period of the sacred truce and invited all Greek citizens to come to Olympia. The first truce is said to have taken place in 776 B.C., the year when history was first recorded in Greece. This year also marked the first of the ancient Olympiads, which took place, without interruption, every four years thereafter for more than a thousand years.

Arranging a truce in the eighth century B.C. between the ancient rivals Elis and Pisa had not been easy. The conflict was so old that no one could remember when it had begun. Many years before, a group of Greek-speaking people, known as Dorians or Doric Greeks, had come down from the European mainland in the north. They had carried iron tools and weapons which were superior to the bronze arms used by the original inhabitants of what we now call Greece. The Doric invaders of the Peloponnesus took over almost all the territory and then reached across the sea and conquered the island of Crete. They settled along the rivers of the Peloponnesus and established city-states like Elis and Sparta. A city-state included the city and the surrounding territory under its control. Some of the original inhabitants of the Peloponnesus, including the citizens of the city-states of Pisa and Messenia, stubbornly defended their homes and lands and clung to their independence. Others were driven into the mountains, where they became mountaineers and shepherds, clinging tenaciously to their ancient customs.

For centuries the bloody conflicts between the old and new city-states raged on. Elis and Pisa remained bitter enemies. There were no natural barriers, such as mountains and deep valleys, to keep them safely separated. The lowland plains around Elis merged imperceptibly into the flat meadows bordering the Alpheus River at Olympia. For years Pisa, just across the river, fought with Elis for control of the Olympic Games.

For countless centuries before 776 B.C., the grove at Olympia had been the scene of athletic festivals. The earliest games probably honored the gods of the fields and the flocks. Chief among the old agricultural goddesses was Hera, the earth mother. Sometimes the early festivals took the form of a suitor's race to win the hand of a princess. Such marriages were often regarded as sacred, symbolizing fruitfulness in nature and expressing hope for the annual flowering of crops and the yearly birth of calves and lambs. Games were also staged at the funerals of great heroes, to celebrate their return to the fruitful earth and to reaffirm the continuation of life after death of a leader.

However, the invading Dorians scoffed at gods of nature who died every fall and winter and were reborn in the spring. Their gods were clad in shining armor and lived forever. They believed that Zeus, the king of the Doric gods, had hurled a lightning bolt into the *altis* at Olympia, dethroned his own father, Cronus, and confined him to the mountainside along the edge of the sacred olive grove. Doric gods were conquerors interested primarily in victory.

Winning in the Olympic Games was believed to be as pleasing to the Doric gods as it was to the princes and spectators assembled to watch the events. Unfairness and corruption were deemed displeasing to the gods; it was considered a sacrilege to violate the rules of the game. A strong bond linked every Greek athlete with his gods, to whom he believed he owed his success. Early competition in Greece was quite free of corruption, particularly at Olympia.

With no athletic events scheduled for the first day of the Olympic Festival, the visitors could wander about and enjoy the magnificent buildings and temples of the *altis*. Along the foot of the Hill of Cronus was a row of buildings called the Treasuries. Each was built by a different Greek city-state to house its prize possessions and to glorify its name and accomplishments.

The main attractions were the Temples of Hera and Zeus. The Temple of Zeus had been built by Libon, an architect from Elis, who began work around 466 B.C. and took ten years to complete the task. Much of the building material for the temple came from the ruins of Pisa, which had finally been conquered and leveled by Elis. Inside the temple, the famous Greek sculptor Phidias had set up his majestic figure of Zeus, the supreme ruler of heaven and earth, seated on his throne. The ivory-and-gold statue was so impressive that it was soon hailed as one of the wonders of the world.

For visitors to the Olympic Games, guides were on hand to conduct tours of the *altis* and describe its art and architecture. Among the visitors there were always great men to be stared at—perhaps a king or a leading statesman. The most famous men of ancient Greece braved the crowds to watch the competitions. The philosophers Plato, Aristotle, and Socrates visited Olympia. Demosthenes, the orator, headed a delegation to Olympia from Athens. Among the poets who wrote about

*Phidias'* Zeus *in the temple of Zeus at Olympia (reconstruction).*
photo German Archaeological Institute, Athens

*Model of Olympia.*  photo German Archaeological Institute, Athens

1 Temple of Zeus   2 Altar of Zeus   3   Temple of Hera
4 Treasuries   5 Bases of *Zanes*  6a Stadium I   6b Stadium II
6c Stadium III   7 Echo Colonnade   8 Judges' Building
9 Council House   10 Leonidaeum   11 Phidias' Workshop
12 *Palaestra*   13 Great Gymnasium   14 Hill of Cronus

the Olympic victors were Pindar, Bacchylides, and Simonides. The historians Thucydides and Herodotus, who wrote the history of the Greek and Persian wars, both attended the Games. Herodotus found a place for himself in the rear portico of the Temple of Zeus and read his history to the crowds. The historian's glorified account of Greek victories charmed his audiences, and his reputation spread throughout the Greek world.

25

A visit to Olympia was not the most comfortable of experiences. The roads were poor and there were few accommodations for visitors. Food could be purchased only from booths and stalls, and drinking water was scarce. Until an ornamental fountain was erected in Roman times, there were only nine freshwater sources to supply the thousands of visitors.

Late summer was a time of fierce, scorching heat by day, barely cooled off by the breezes at night. The noise and din of thousands of people crammed into the *altis* overpowered the stillness of the sanctuary. Taking baths was a problem, despite moments of sudden, drenching downpours, which soaked visitors to the skin. Conditions were so uncomfortable that one Greek master threatened to punish his disobedient slave by sending him to Olympia to endure all its hardships.

On the other hand, visitors were delighted by the spectacle of the Games. Almost everyone agreed with the Greek satirist Lucian, who told a skeptical visitor from Scythia:

> My dear Anacharsis, if it were time for the Olympic Games, or the Isthmian or Panathenaic Games, the events there would themselves teach you that the energy we give to athletics is not wasted. But telling you how delightful the Games are will not really convince you. You should sit there yourself, among the spectators, and see the fine contestants, how beautiful and healthy their bodies are, their marvelous skill and unbeatable strength, their daring and ambition, their firm resolve and their absolute will to win. I know quite well that you would never stop praising them, clapping and cheering.

In the middle of the fourth century B.C., a special building called the Leonidaeum would provide a residence for distinguished guests. A gymnasium would be used as accommoda-

*Javelin thrower with trainer. Red-figured bowl, sixth century B.C.*

Museo Nazionale Tarquiniese, photo Hirmer Fotoarchiv, Munich

tion for the athletes. In the meantime, the competitors had to train and practice in the open air and live in a crowded bath house, which they shared with their trainers, officials, and important visitors. The fields outside the olive grove were crowded with tents and with hastily constructed wooden huts, which served as sleeping quarters for a fortunate few. Most of the spectators at Olympia had to sleep in the open, under the stars. The *altis* was a residence for gods, not men.

27

THE ANCIENT GREEK WORLD

# THE SECOND DAY

## THE CHARIOT RACES

Early in the morning of the second day of the Olympic Festival, the low embankments around the Hippodrome began to fill up with crowds eager to see the chariot and horse races. Spectators pushed and shoved, elbowing their way to their favorite vantage points. The choicest spots were at either end of the racetrack, facing the pillars around which the horses and chariots had to make their sharp turns. As they jostled one another, the men—young and old—talked at the top of their voices. No one wore a hat as protection from the scorching sun, because it was forbidden to block anyone's view of the race.

Very soon the procession, which had assembled in the *altis,* came into view, headed as usual by the purple-robed judges with garlands of olive branches on their heads. They were followed by the heralds, the trumpeters, and other officials. Then came the charioteers, driving their teams, and the riders, astride their horses. As the competitors passed before the judges' stand, a herald called out the name of each horse-and-chariot owner, his father, and his city. The herald then asked if anybody had charges against any of the competitors.

The chariots were wheeled into their places in the stalls of the *aphesis*, or starting gate, each of which had been assigned by the drawing of lots. Chariot owners often strolled about in the crowd, clad in rich garments and fancy jewelry. They usually were the aristocrats or the wealthy citizens of a community, sometimes even the king or ruling tyrant. Sometimes a racing vehicle was owned by a woman, even though women were not allowed to be present in the sacred precinct at Olympia.

*Chariot and driver, bronze statuette; and four-horse chariot, black-figured amphora; both sixth century B.C.*

Olympia Museum, photo N.A. Tombazi; The Metropolitan Museum of Art, Fletcher Fund, 1956

The chariot race recalled one of the oldest Greek legends. It celebrated a legendary competition between an ancient king of Pisa, Oenomaus, whose name meant "the wine drinker," and Pelops, a suitor for the hand of his daughter, the princess Hippodamia. Oenomaus had learned from an oracle that he would lose his life at the hand of a prospective son-in-law. The only way he could escape the oracle's prediction was to prevent his daughter from marrying. The king challenged every suitor for Hippodamia's hand to a chariot race. The young man would have to win or else be put to death. The old king made sure no suitor would beat him; he slyly arranged to have his beautiful daughter ride in her suitor's chariot, knowing that her presence would distract the youth and keep him from concentrating on the race. King Oenomaus even let his youthful rival have a head start in the race, because he knew how fast his own horses were and how skillfully his charioteer, Myrtilus, could handle them.

Whenever the king in his chariot overtook the youthful suitor, he immediately ran him through with a spear and killed him. The heads of the victims were nailed to the wall over the entrance to the palace, a sight grim enough to frighten away most potential sons-in-law.

Twelve times young hopefuls had raced against King Oenomaus and twelve times they had lost and died. Pelops, however, was not discouraged by the fate of his predecessors. Yet he took a few precautions of his own to insure his victory. Learning that the king's charioteer was secretly in love with Hippodamia but too timid to compete for her openly, Pelops promised him that Hippodamia would return his love for one night if he would remove the bronze pins from the wheels on the king's chariot and replace them with wax.

Hippodamia dutifully climbed into the chariot beside Pelops and immediately fell in love with him. For the first time, she wanted her suitor to overcome her father. With Hippodamia at his side, Pelops started off in the race, urging his horses on with his whip. Their hooves pounded the earth, the chariot wheels spun around swiftly, but behind him Pelops could hear the king's chariot thundering nearer and nearer, gaining ground with every passing second. Suddenly, the wax pins in the king's chariot melted and the wheels flew off. Oenomaus was thrown to the ground, and Pelops overpowered and slew him, winning both the princess and the king's throne. When Oenomaus' charioteer demanded his reward, Pelops tossed him into the sea, eliminating both a rival for Hippodamia and a witness to his own plot.

In another, more ancient account of the race, Pelops had been given a golden chariot by Poseidon, the god of the sea, who also provided him with four winged horses to draw the magic vehicle. When King Oenomaus saw the glittering chariot, his heart grew fearful, but he could not withdraw from the race. The king's

*Hippodamia and Pelops. Red-figured amphora, fifth century* B.C.

33

horses were swift, possibly even swifter than Poseidon's. Oenomaus seemed to be winning the race, when the sea god intervened again and cast a spell on the king's chariot so that the wheels came off and the king was thrown to his death. In the meantime, Pelops sped on alone and crossed the finish line to win. When he looked back, he saw that the royal palace had been struck by a bolt of lightning and was burning fiercely. Pelops swung his chariot around and raced back, arriving just in time to rescue Hippodamia from the flames.

Visitors to Olympia would have had good reason to accept the story of the fiery destruction of King Oenomaus' palace. A wooden pillar in the *altis*, near the altar to Zeus, was believed to have survived the legendary fire. It was described by a Roman traveler and writer, Pausanias, who saw it on his visit to Olympia in the second century A.D. The pillar was very old, its timber held together by iron clamps. Fastened to it was a small bronze tablet with the inscription:

> Stranger, I am the last
> survivor of a once-proud house;
> I was a tall
> column in the halls of Oenomaus.
>
> Now bound fast, I lie
> near Zeus. O I am worth
> your admiration! I alone
> the all-devouring fire did not burn.

However, no trace of any palace inhabited by King Oenomaus has been unearthed near Olympia in modern times.

The Hippodrome, where the equestrian events of the Olympic Games were staged, lay beyond the *altis*, toward the place where the Alpheus River and its wild tributary, the Cladeus, met. The racing arena was a large, flat, open space, rectangular in shape, twice the length of the stadium. The racecourse was straight and level, with turning posts at either end of the track. The four-horse chariot race measured about 5⅓ miles, 24 times the length of the Hippodrome.

The starting gate for the chariot race resembled the prow of a ship, with its narrow end pointing toward the course. Before the gate was an altar with a bronze eagle and a center pole, on which a bronze dolphin perched. Each charioteer took his place in a trap that had a rope stretched across its front. A blast of the trumpet signaled to the spectators that the race was about to start. The dolphin toppled from its perch and the eagle soared into the air. At the same time, the ropes in the traps were lowered, starting with the ones farthest back, one set at a time, until the whole field formed a straight line at the starting position. The trumpeter blew another blast of his horn, and the chariot race began.

Horses and chariots were off, running in short bursts, interrupted by violent turns around the poles at each end of the track. The light carts bounced and swerved, often bumping into one another around the full 180-degree turns. There were no barriers between the chariots racing in opposite directions, so head-on collisions often occurred.

The finishing post of the chariot race recalled the legendary origin of the contest. On the post was a representation of Hippodamia binding a fillet of wool on the brow of Pelops. At Olympia, the winner's crown—a wreath of olive branches—went to the owner of the victorious chariot and horses. The winning charioteer had to be content with a headband of ram's wool.

The first Olympic chariot race for teams of four horses was staged in 680 B.C. for the 25th Olympiad. It represented the growing interest in horse breeding for military purposes and also fulfilled the desire of the older, wealthier aristocracy to

*Winning athlete
crowning himself.
Marble relief, fifth century B.C.*

National Museum, Athens, photo N.A. Tombazi

take part in the Olympics, since foot races, wrestling, boxing, and the discus and javelin throws were only for men in their full athletic prime.

Among the entrants in the first Olympic chariot race was a nobleman from Thebes, named Pagondas. His rivals were owners from Sparta, Elis, Athens, and other Greek city-states and overseas colonies. At the sound of the trumpet, as the bronze eagle "flew" into the air, the chariots sped off with each driver shouting to his team and pulling the reins in his hands. Dust flew up in a great cloud and the noise of the wheels filled the Hippodrome. Each driver goaded his team without mercy, trying to keep his axles clear and his panting steeds from colliding with a rival. The horses' breath steamed in the morning air. Their backs were soon drenched with sweat. Foam flecked their straining mouths.

The beginning of the race was comparatively slow, as the chariots, sometimes numbering as many as forty, raced up and down the Hippodrome. Sometimes the charioteers drove forward recklessly, avoiding collisions by a hair's breadth. At other times, horses, carts, and drivers piled up in a tangle of utter confusion. The cautious driver pulled aside when disaster threatened and waited until the course was clear again. Up and back the light chariots wheeled, while the excitement of the onlookers mounted.

The driver of Pagondas' chariot used his whip without let-up, lashing out at the middle pair, harnessed to the chariot pole, and at the outside two, running alongside freely as trace horses. The chariot was low slung, a light platform mounted on an axle, without springs. There were only two small wheels, each with four spokes. Larger wheels would have permitted the chariots to go faster, but the small ones were safer on the rough, uneven track. The driver stood in his low cart, the framework about as high as his knees on three sides, the rear open.

For a while every chariot rolled along without mishap until, at the sharp turn, one team suddenly took the bit in its mouth and ran head-on into another. The accident led to other collisions, and the racecourse became a sea of wrecked chariots. Pagondas' driver had seen what was happening and had drawn aside, biding his time and keeping clear of the wrecks. With effort he held his team back. Then with only one rival left, he shouted to his horses and urged them on with his long whip. The two teams raced side by side, first one, then the other forging ahead into the lead. At the final turn, Pagondas' charioteer reined in his inner trace horse, giving the outer one its head with such skill that the hub of his wheel just cleared the post.

The spectators on either embankment along the Hippodrome were wild with excitement as the trumpeter blew the signal for the last half lap, a straight gallop to the finishing post —and victory for Pagondas' chariot.

When the race was over, the herald proclaimed the names of the victor, his father, and the city he represented. Pagondas stepped forward. He walked proudly to the judges' stand, leading the chariot, while the spectators showered him with flowers and branches. A fillet of wool was tied around the forehead of his charioteer. For his own prize, the Theban nobleman would be given an olive crown cut from the sacred tree.

According to the rules, if the race had ended in a tie, the olive crown would have been dedicated to the gods.

Spartan noblemen were particularly proud of their skill as horse breeders and racers. In 548 B.C. Eugoras of Sparta won the chariot race, then repeated the feat with the same team of horses in the next two Olympiads.

The noble owners did not always entrust their chariots to hired drivers. In 504 B.C. King Demaratus of Sparta actually handled the reins himself and won.

Winners of the four-horse chariot race often figured prominently in ancient Greek history. Cimon of Athens won with his team in three successive Olympiads, beginning in 536 B.C. Cimon was the father of Miltiades, the famous general who led the Greeks to victory over the invading Persians at Marathon in 490 B.C.

In 488 B.C. a four-horse chariot was entered by Gelon, the ruler of Gela, who had also extended his power over Syracuse in Sicily. Twenty years later, his brother, Hieron, who succeeded him as tyrant of Syracuse, also won the major chariot race at Olympia.

In the 90th Olympiad in 420 B.C., a member of the royal family of Sparta, named Lichas, entered his four-horse chariot. His father, Arcesilaus, had won the chariot race twice, and the younger man was eager to match his father's prowess. But, since Sparta had been barred from the competition because it was accused of violating the truce, Lichas disguised himself as a Boeotian. Lichas' team romped in to win the race, and he was so overcome by excitement that he leaped onto the track to claim his crown. He was recognized as a Spartan and beaten out of the Hippodrome with whips. The Spartans did not forget or forgive. As soon as they could, they defeated Elis in battle and restored Lichas' name to the list of Olympic winners.

In 416 B.C. Alcibiades, the brilliant naval commander of Athens, entered seven chariots in the four-horse race and won first and second places, with another of his chariots coming in fourth. To celebrate this feat he borrowed all the urns, bowls, and other gold and silver vessels in the Athenian Treasury for a personal victory banquet.

The kings and statesmen who sent their fastest horses and chariots to Olympia were often interested in matters other than sport. Dionysius I, the tyrant of Syracuse, entered the competition with several teams of horses, all faster than those of his competitors. He also set up a colorful tent, interwoven with gold and outfitted with luxurious carpets. Dionysius considered himself a poet, and he wanted to attract as large an audience as possible to his tent for his poetry readings. People flocked to admire the splendid horses, but they laughed at his poor verses and knocked over his magnificent tent.

Since chariot owners did not have to handle the reins personally, women were not prevented from entering the competition, even though they were forbidden to attend the event. The teams of Cynisca, daughter of the king of Sparta, won twice, proving that she was a first-rate trainer and breeder. She had a bronze statue of her horses erected in the *altis*.

Other women who won were Euryleonis of Sparta, with a chariot drawn by two horses, and Belistiche, the first owner to win the chariot race with two colts, which was added to the Olympic program in 264 B.C. In the first century A.D., the chariot race for four young horses was run for the first time, and Theodota of Elis won.

Some chariots were owned publicly by an entire community. A collectively owned team from Dyspontium won in 672 B.C. In 472 B.C. the four-horse chariot owned by the city-state of Argos beat eleven competitors.

In time, still other equestrian events were added to the Olympic program. In 500 B.C., for the 70th Olympiad, a chariot race with four mules was introduced. For this race the charioteer did not stand but sat in the rolling carriage. The event never became truly popular and was soon abandoned. When chariot races for two-horse teams were instituted toward the end of the fifth century B.C., the first winner's crown went to a team from Elis. Soon afterward, in 384 B.C., a chariot race with a team of four colts was run for the first time. Twelve years later this event was won by Troilus of Elis, who also happened to be one of the judges, whereupon a new regulation forbidding judges to compete in chariot or horse races was immediately adopted. In 268 B.C. a chariot race with paired colts was still another addition to the program.

By the time the chariot races were over, the surface of the track in the Hippodrome had been churned up by the horses' hooves.

As the morning hours passed, the heat of the day mounted. A cloud of dust hung over the excited crowds as they waited eagerly for the next events.

# THE HORSE RACES

The first horse race was for fully grown stallions—skittish, high-spirited steeds. They ran twice the length of the Hippodrome, a total distance of nearly half a mile. Horse racing in ancient Greece was a sport for the glory of the owners. The horse owners, like the sponsors of the chariot races, rarely competed in the race in person. Instead they hired jockeys, who had to ride without saddle or stirrup. Horses were unshod, as metal shoes were still unknown. The bridle was a plain, slender bit, without a curb, which fitted into the horse's mouth. The rider could only control the horse by the pressure of his knees, by maneuvering the reins, or by wielding his whip.

The horse race had been introduced in 648 B.C., more than thirty years after the first competition for chariots. This first race was won by a spirited stallion owned by Crauxidas from Crannon in Thessaly. In the 67th Olympiad, in 512 B.C., a mare named Breeze was entered in a race by her owner, Phidolas of Corinth. The fiery mare was maneuvered into the starting gate. Just as the race got under way, however, Breeze threw her

*Horse race. Black-figured amphora, fifth century B.C.*
British Museum

jockey, but she continued to race down the track. Turning sharply around the post, and hearing the trumpet blow the signal for the last lap, she quickened her stride and sped across the finish line first. Even without her rider, Breeze was declared the winner, and Phidolas was awarded the prize. His sons carried on their father's racing tradition, winning the race in the next Olympiad in 508 B.C., with a horse called Wolf.

Horse racing continued to be a sport of Greek kings and rulers. In 476 B.C., Hieron, the ruler of the Greek colony of Syracuse, sponsored the winning stallion, and four years later another charger from his stables won the olive wreath for him.

The Macedonians, whose home was in northeastern Greece, were regarded by the Greeks as foreigners, but they proved themselves eligible to participate in the Olympic Games by claiming direct descent from Hercules. In 356 B.C., King Philip II of Macedonia entered his favorite stallion in the Olympics, and it won. News of the horse's success reached Philip on the same day that he received two other heartwarming reports. His army had won a military victory, and his wife had given birth to a son, who was named Alexander, later to become known as Alexander the Great. Even as he extended his empire, Alexander always kept his interest in athletics. He refused to compete in the Olympic Games, however, because not all his opponents would be kings.

# THE *PENTATHLON*: *Five Events*

When the last race in the Hippodrome was over, the spectators hurried to the stadium to watch the athletes compete

*Three pentathletes: discus and javelin throwers, and wrestler. Red-figured amphora, fifth century B.C.*

in all five events of the *pentathlon*. The pentathlete was considered the most attractive of all Greek youths. He had an ideal figure—slim, of medium height, with well-developed torso and leg muscles. His legs were long enough for the stade race and the long jump, his back flexible enough for hurling the javelin and the discus. Long hands and slender fingers gave him the proper grip for throwing the discus and the javelin. His whole body was put to the test in the upright wrestling competition.

The five events of the *pentathlon*—the discus throw, long jump, javelin throw, stade race, and upright wrestling—were a basic part of the education of all Greek boys and sometimes,

43

in Sparta, of girls. The discus—from the Greek word *diskos*, meaning a thing for throwing—could have been any of the round stones which had been smoothed by the water along the country's coast line. Dumbbells and throwing weights were fashioned into discuses by young people training in gymnasia. The discus was thrown for distance.

Greece, a country of streams and ditches, was ideal territory for developing the long, or broad, jump. With no fences or hedges, the land offered little inspiration for a high jump.

The contest with the javelin was a reminder of times of hunting and warfare. With the addition of the stade race, already a feature of the Olympic Games, and upright wrestling, the oldest and most widely practiced of ancient sports, the program of the *pentathlon* was complete.

The *pentathlon* was the only competition in which placing second or third was important. A combination of second- and third-place victories in the different events could still add up to a victor's crown.

Aristotle and other Greek writers were lavish in their praise of the pentathlete's all-around ability. Their words could have described young Lampis of Sparta, who entered the first *pentathlon* in 708 B.C. for the 18th Olympiad.


## DISCUS THROW

For the first event of the *pentathlon*, the discus throw; the contestants assembled around a small area, called the *balbis*, at one end of the stadium. The *balbis* was marked off by a stone starting line and by rows of pegs on either side. There was no line in the rear of the *balbis*, so the thrower could take as many steps as he pleased before releasing the discus.

Lampis waited patiently near the *balbis*. He carried a bronze discus on his shoulder. He rubbed the discus with fine sand so that he could get a firm grip. One of the contestants was about to complete his first discus throw. His body strained to bring the utmost force behind the throw. Lampis wondered whether the simple style of his rival, requiring only one step, might be more effective than his own, which needed three. Each contestant in the discus throw had five chances. A judge marked the best of the throws with a peg.

When his turn came, Lampis took his place on the *balbis*. His right foot was forward, bearing his weight. Holding the discus in his left hand, he let it swing forward and took it in his right. Then as the discus arced vigorously down and back, he bent his body to the right, turning his head so that he could see the right side of his body. Then, putting the whole force of his body into the movement, Lampis threw the discus. His throw was timed to the rhythm of flute music. The young Spartan saw the pegs set down by the judge and

*Discus thrower, jumper, and flute player. Black-figured amphora, sixth century B.C.*

University of Würzburg,
Martin von Wagner-Museum

45

knew that he had done better than any of his competitors.

Years later other discus throwers in the Olympic competitions performed feats that became legends. One, named Phlegyas, amused himself by throwing a discus across the widest stretch of the Alpheus River, some 55 to 65 yards across. According to all the stories told about him, never once did the discus fall into the river.


## LONG JUMP

After the discus throw, the pentathletes competed in a second event—the long jump. In Greece, jumping was not a military exercise, because Greek soldiers were so encumbered by armor and heavy weapons that they were unable to perform feats of agility. The long jump was an amusement of peacetime, a part of rhythmic, physical training. It was very much like dancing and, as with the discus throw, was performed to flute music.

The athletes took their places near a stone sill, called a *bater*, which provided leverage for the jump. The jumping area was marked off by a row of spears stuck in the ground. In front was a landing area called a *skamma*, an area of earth about 50 feet long, broken up and raked smooth to provide a soft landing carpet. The smooth earth would also take a clear imprint of the jumper's feet when he landed.

In their hands, Lampis and the other contestants held jumping weights called *halteres*, heavy semicircular dumbbells which would help the jumpers keep their balance and also make their landings in the pit sharp and clean. The *halteres* were made of various materials—lead, iron, or stone. They were of different shapes, sizes, and weights.

*Jumper with weights, and judge. Red-figured wine cup, fifth century* B.C.

Lampis gripped his jumping weights tightly, his fingers fastening around the grooves cut in the lower side. He swung his arms forward until they were at shoulder height. Then his arms flew back and down; his body bent until his hands were just below his knees. As his arms swung forward, he made his actual jump. The rhythm of the swing was timed to the flute music played by a figure in a long, flowing robe.

As Lampis landed in the *skamma*, he swung the weights backward with considerable force to keep himself from toppling over. His landing had to be sharp and distinct. If the imprint of his feet in the earth was not clear, the jump would not be marked. Also, if he stumbled or fell, or if he landed with one foot ahead of the other, the jump would be judged invalid.

Lampis could not only do the long jump from a standing position but was also adept at leaping from a running start.

At one time the jumping contest might have consisted of five leaps in sequence. This is the only way to explain how another Spartan athlete, named Chionis, is said to have jumped 52 feet in the Olympic Games of 664 B.C.

47

# JAVELIN THROW

The third event in the *pentathlon* was throwing the javelin, a straight pole about 6 feet long and as thick as an average man's finger. Lampis had been taught two ways of throwing the javelin. He used a throwing loop, called an *amentum*, which he rolled around the shaft of the javelin. When hurling for distance, he attached the loop near the end of the shaft. When aiming at a target, Lampis would throw more accurately with the throwing loop fastened farther forward on the shaft. For distance, the javelin would have a blunt,

*Jumper, javelin and discus throwers, practicing. Black-figured oil jug, sixth century B.C.*

The Metropolitan Museum of Art, Rogers Fund, 1906

weighted cap on the end. For accuracy, he used a sharpened point so that it would become fixed in the target.

Lampis had brought his own throwing loop to Olympia, and now he fitted it onto the shaft of the javelin handed to him for the competition. He tightened the thong and tested it to be sure that it was positioned just where he wanted it.

Lampis put his index and middle fingers in the loop, letting the javelin itself rest on his thumb. The use of the loop would increase the force of the throw and send the javelin through the air with a spinning motion, which would keep it steady in flight.

Unlike the warrior or hunter, who dared not take his eyes off his quarry, Lampis turned his head backward to watch the weapon in his hand, concentrating the force of his whole body behind the throw. His movement was rhythmic, timed to flute music.

The young athlete from Sparta could not be sure just how well he was doing in the *pentathlon.* Three events had taken place, and he was confident that he had won one of them. But how had he scored in the other two?


## STADE RACE

The athletes assembled for the fourth event of the *pentathlon*—the stade race, a sprint down the length of the stadium. Lampis and the other competitors took their positions at the starting line. At the signal, they were off, speeding down the field, running lightly and swiftly over the sandy ground.

Considered the classic event of the Olympic Games, the stade race would be run as a separate event on the morning of the fourth day.

# UPRIGHT WRESTLING

The fifth and last event of the *pentathlon* was a wrestling match, which was held in the *altis* before the altar of Zeus. Wrestling was a difficult exercise that depended on skill and agility as well as physical strength. *Pentathlon* wrestlers could not rely on brute force alone to overpower their opponents.

Like the other contestants, Lampis rubbed his body with oil and dabbed it with sand. Each athlete carried his oil in a small flask. After each competition he would scrape the oil and dust off with his *strigil*. Now Lampis faced his opponent,

*Athletes, each with* strigil *and oil jar. Red-figured vase, fifth century* B.C.

*Wrestlers watched by a goddess. Detail of red-figured vase, fifth century B.C.*

cautiously circling him and searching for an opportunity to get a grip on him. He made a feint, drawing his opponent off balance, then quickly moved in, caught his rival in a tight hold, and threw him to the ground. He did this a second time, then a third. Lampis had won! Three falls were required to win the wrestling match.

With his victory in the upright wrestling match, Lampis became the first pentathlete winner in the Olympic Games. Thirty-two years later, in the 26th Olympiad in 676 B.C., another Spartan youth, Philombrotus, won the *pentathlon.* He repeated this feat twice more in the next two Olympic Games.

The sun sank lower and lower toward the western horizon. The horse races and chariot races, followed by the five events of the *pentathlon*, had provided an exciting day for the thousands of spectators at Olympia.

51

# THE THIRD DAY

THE FULL MOON hung in the velvet sky over the *altis* as night ushered in the third round of Festival activities at Olympia. Sounds of celebration, music, laughter, and rejoicing could be heard as the winning chariot owners, proudly wreathed in fillets and garlands, feasted their friends. Banquets were also in progress for the victorious pentathletes. Processions wound around the *altis* to the sound of the flute and the lyre. The feasting and revelry went on until the early morning. The revelers sang songs of triumph and recited poems.

*Athletes in procession. Black-figured amphora, sixth century B.C.*
British Museum

Some of the songs celebrated ancient victories by Hercules. Others were inspired by memories of ancient sports and games held in honor of the triumph of a god, the adventure of a hero, or the funeral of a king or a chieftain, who, it was thought, would enjoy the spectacle even beyond the grave.

The poets Pindar and Bacchylides celebrated the Pan-Hellenic Games and immortalized the victors in lordly verse. The first lines of Pindar's *Olympian Ode I* express the superiority of the Olympic Festival:

> Water is most excellent
> of earthly things. Of splendid wealth,
> gold shines brightest, like fire
> glowing in darkness.
>
> O my soul, shall we sing of crowns
> and contests? Then know this—
>
> The sun warms more than any lesser star,
> and no festival outshines Olympia.

# THE SACRIFICE TO ZEUS

In the morning of the third day of the Olympic Festival came the most solemn ritual of all—the official sacrifice to Zeus. Early that morning a procession formed, once again headed by the purple-robed Hellanodicae. They were followed by priests and attendants and a herd of a hundred bulls to be sacrificed. Next came the sacred embassies, the official representatives of the various Greek city-states, each carrying vessels of silver and gold, gifts to Zeus. After them came the charioteers and horsemen, the athletes and their trainers, kinsmen and friends.

The procession wound past the Temple of Zeus and made its way through an avenue of statues to the Great Altar. The Great Altar was a mound of ashes 20 feet high, piled-up remains of sacrifices made over countless years. The altar was set in the midst of the *altis*, close to the spot which Zeus had made sacred with his thunderbolt. The priests of Zeus, attended by seers and ministers, mounted a platform set close to the altar and, in full view of the assembled crowd, sacrificed the herd. The cattle's thighs were taken to the top of the mound and burned, adding to the pile of ashes. The rest of the meat was taken to the central building, the Magistrates' House, for the victory banquet which would conclude the Olympic Games.

# BOYS' EVENTS

The sacrifices and ceremonies were over by noon, and the rest of the third day was devoted to the boys' events. These were events for youths over seventeen years of age, but under twenty. Included were many of the events staged for older athletes: the stade race, wrestling, boxing, and eventually the *pankration*, a combination of boxing and wrestling.

Sports events for boys were introduced into the Olympic Festival in 632 B.C., for the 37th Olympiad, when two competitions were staged—the stade race, a sprint down the length of the stadium, and a wrestling match. The boys' sprint was won for the first time by Polynices of Elis.

*Pancratiasts and trainer. Red-figured wine cup, fifth century* B.C.

The *pentathlon* was staged for boys, but only once—in the 38th Olympiad in 628 B.C. It was won by Eutelidas of Sparta. That afternoon Eutelidas rubbed off the oil and grime on his body with his *strigil*, refreshed himself, and proceeded to win another event—the boys' wrestling match.

Olympic legends grew up even around the boys' events. In the 46th Olympiad, held in 596 B.C., the winner of the stade race was Polymestor of Miletus, a shepherd so fleet of foot he supposedly could outrun a hare and capture it with his bare hands.

The winner of the first boys' wrestling match was a Spartan youth named Hipposthenes. Four years later, Hipposthenes tried to win the same event again but failed. Eight years later, he entered the men's wrestling competition and won. He ultimately went on to win a total of six olive wreaths. His son, Hetoemocles, also became an Olympic wrestling champion, probably winning the boys' event in 592 B.C. As a man, Hetoemocles followed Hipposthenes' footsteps to win a total of five Olympic victories, just one fewer than his father.

Upright wrestling in ancient Greece was an exercise in style and grace. A wrestler required special training. The role of the trainer was recognized as an important one. The statue of one trainer, Cratinus, was set up alongside that representing his victorious pupil. Spartan wrestlers, however, did not have trainers because they had little regard for wrestling, either as a sport or as physical exercise.

Spartan athletes prided themselves on their force rather than skill, as one boastful youth was said to have written: "The other wrestlers are stylists. I win by my strength, as is only right and fitting for a Spartan youth."

Contests between boy athletes pleased the bustling crowds at Olympia. For the 41st Olympiad, staged in 616 B.C., the boxing contest was introduced and with it, all of the excitement, brutality, and bloodshed that characterized the adult matches. The first winner was Philyatis, a youth from Sybaris, a wealthy Greek colony in Italy. (The English word *sybarite* means a lover of luxury and magnificence.)

About the end of the fifth century B.C., Pisirodus, the youngest member of an illustrious family of Olympic champions, entered the boys' boxing contest. His grandfather was Diagoras of Rhodes, perhaps the most celebrated of all Olympic boxers. Three of his uncles were also Olympic champions, winners of the *pankration* and boxing events. His cousin, Eucles of Rhodes, entered the men's boxing contest during the same Festival (the 94th Olympiad—404 B.C.) and was considered likely to win.

Pisirodus' mother, Callipatira, was eager for her son to live up to her family's reputation. Since her husband was dead, she decided to defy the ban on women at the Olympic Games and go disguised as a trainer for her son. Young Pisirodus fulfilled all of his family's hopes by battering his way to victory in the boys' boxing match. His mother was so overjoyed at his triumph, she leaped over a barricade to get to the field. During the jump, her cloak opened, and it was revealed that she was a woman. The Olympic judges were deeply angered.

The penalty for a woman who broke the law and entered the *altis* was a particularly unpleasant death—the woman was to be cast off a mountain across from the Alpheus River. The judges would have ordered this awful death for Callipatira, but in honor of her father and brothers, who had won Olympic immortality, she was pardoned. A decree was issued that thereafter all trainers at the Olympic Games, like the athletes, were to appear totally nude so that women would not dare show themselves.

Boy competitors sometimes found it difficult to prove their eligibility for the Games. Since birth certificates were unknown, the judges could only guess at a boy's age from his physical development.

In the 48th Olympiad in 588 B.C., a youthful figure from Samos, a Greek island off the coast of Asia Minor, presented himself to the judges as a competitor in the boys' boxing match. His name was Pythagoras. The judges were startled by his appearance. Pythagoras arrived wearing great purple robes, with long hair hanging loose around his shoulders. Physically he seemed too developed for a boy, so the judges rejected his bid to fight in the junior matches. Pythagoras thereupon entered the men's boxing competition the following day, and won. He was, perhaps, the first Olympic athlete to overcome the blundering, brute strength of his opponents with speed and with skill.

*Girl athlete in the Heraea.*
*Roman copy of Greek statue,*
*fifth century B.C.*

Although girls were not permitted to participate in the Games, girl athletes did compete in a series of foot races staged in non-Olympic years. The games for girls were organized by sixteen matrons from Elis who had originally been selected, it was believed, by Hippodamia, in gratitude to Hera for her marriage to Pelops. The contests were called the Heraea, in honor of the queen of the gods, the wife and sister of Zeus.

The girl contestants, divided into three age groups, competed over a distance one-sixth shorter than the stade race for men. The girls wore short tunics that reached just above their knees. Their hair flowed down their backs, their right shoulders were bared to the breast. They were crowned with wild olive wreaths, like victors in the Olympic Games.

As the afternoon waned, the new boy Olympic champions were regarded with eager interest by the watching crowds. Any one of them might go on to win the men's events in an Olympiad to come.

# THE FOURTH DAY

## THE FOOT RACES: *Three Events*

Dawn. The sun peering over the eastern horizon glistened on the faces of the crowds rushing to find places in the stadium. It was the morning of the fourth day of the Olympic Games. All the remaining athletic events were scheduled for that day, so it was important to get to the stadium early to get a place. There could be as many as 40,000 others milling around, looking for a favorable spot.

The purple-robed judges were in a special stand along the edge of the embankment that separated the stadium from the Hippodrome. Across from the racetrack, halfway down its length, was an altar for Demeter, the goddess of agriculture. During the Games the altar was attended by a priestess—the only woman allowed in the *altis.*

### LONG RACE (*Dolichos*)

The sun rose over the rim of the mountains as the first race got under way. It was a long-distance event—called the *dolichos*, meaning literally the "long racecourse"—which covered the length of the stadium 20 times, a distance of about 2¼ miles. The race was unexciting until the last few moments, so it was scheduled as the first event of the day to give the crowd a chance to assemble. By starting the morning's events with the "long race," the program also allowed time for the spectators to wake up after their night of revelry or worship and gradually find places along the sides of the stadium.

The *dolichos* had not always been the first of the foot races to be run. When it was added to the program, for the 15th Olympiad in 720 B.C., it was the last of the running events. Visitors from Corinth at this Olympiad were especially excited about the *dolichos* because there was still a chance for victory in the new event.

Beyond Corinth, farther east along the peninsula leading to the Greek mainland, was a rival seaport, Megara. Both cities were busy commercial centers; both had established colonies in Sicily. Their rivalry extended to athletic competitions. Orhippus of Megara had already won the stade race. His eyes fixed on the finishing post, 600 feet from the starting line, Orhippus had thought of nothing but the race. He had not realized that halfway down the path his loincloth had worked itself loose and fallen off. And even though the disgruntled Corinthians had grumbled about the unfair advantage of running without the hindrance of a girdle, he had been named the victor. In the second event of the day, the double stade race, or *diaulos*, both the Corinthian and the Megarian runners had lost.

But there was still a third chance for a crown in that 15th Olympiad. The competitors from Corinth, Elis, Pisa, Sparta, and Megara took their positions. The Spartan athlete entered in the new event was named Acanthus.

At the blast of the trumpet, the runners were off, their bodies gleaming in the sun, their leather girdles, or loincloths,

*Runners in the long race. Detail of black-figured vase, fourth century B.C.*
British Museum

flapping lightly around their waists. Acanthus ran smoothly and easily with the other competitors, displaying a running style quite different from that of the sprinters. He held his arms high and close to his body, as though conserving his strength for the long distance. His arms swung rhythmically as his legs moved in long, sweeping strides. He held his chest out and his head high as he sped along on the balls of his feet.

61

Ten times around the stadium the runners kept up the smooth, steady pace. Finally, as they turned into the nineteenth lap, the trumpet blew the signal for the last stretch—a sprint to the finish line.

As the Spartan rounded the pole, heading for the final sprint to the finish, he could see, out of the corner of his eye, rival runners just a few steps behind him. With a flash he stripped off his girdle and let it fly off to the side. Now naked, he sped toward the finish line and streaked across it, just steps ahead of his nearest competitor. The Spartan had won the day's third crown of olive branches.

From that day on, contenders in the ancient Olympic Games wore no clothing during competition.

Although the sprints and the long-distance races required different kinds of training, there were a few triple victors, or *triastai*, in the ancient Olympic races. Polites of Caria won all three foot races in the 212th Olympiad. The most famous *triastes* of all was Leonidas of Rhodes, who won three olive crowns in four successive Olympiads, from 164 B.C. to 152 B.C.

One long-distance runner, Dromeus of Stymphalus, who won twice at Olympia, convinced the Hellanodicae in Elis to add meat to the training diet of the athletes. He maintained that to keep up his endurance he needed richer food than cheese and figs.

The endurance of long-distance runners is glorified in the legendary exploits of some of the Olympic champions. According to legend, Ageus of Argos, winner of the long run in the 113th Olympiad in 328 B.C., received his olive crown and immediately set out at a run for his home 60 miles away, as the crow flies, reaching his destination that very same day. Drymus of Epidaurus is said to have run even farther—90 miles across the mountains of the Peloponnesus to his home on the eastern shore in a single day.

# STADE RACE

The morning sun climbed upward in the heavens as the runners lined up for the major event—the sprint down the length of the stadium. The spectators, crowding on the sidelines, craned their necks for a glimpse of the trim figures waiting near the stone starting line for the trumpeter's signal. Who would have his name linked to this Olympiad and win immortality for himself and his city-state?

For the first fifty-two years of the historic Olympiads the stade race was the only event in the Games. The stade race was a short sprint of 600 feet down the length of the stadium, the distance Hercules was said to have paced out in days long gone. Originally, when the Olympic Games were merely a local festival lasting only one day, this race was run at noon, right after the sacrifices on the Great Altar to Zeus.

At the first recorded Olympic Games, in 776 B.C., there had been only one judge—Iphitus, the king of Elis. Iphitus had asked the Oracle of Delphi for advice on how to end Elis' war with the neighboring city-state Pisa. The priestess at Delphi had advised King Iphitus to revive the Games at Olympia. It had been difficult for King Iphitus to convince King Cleosthenes of Pisa to accept a truce after so many years of battle and bloodshed. But, in 776 B.C., the truce was agreed upon and its sacred character guaranteed by another important figure of a Peloponnesian state—Lycurgus, the lawmaker of Sparta.

King Iphitus, wrapped in a purple cloak, had presided over those first Games. His military leaders who hovered nearby had seemed uneasy without their weapons. By the terms of the sacred truce, all arms were forbidden at Olympia.

Not far from Zeus' altar a throne-like chair had been set up for King Iphitus to judge the foot race. The running track was at that time quite close to the center of the *altis.* During

63

later centuries it was moved twice, each time farther away from the altar.

Among the runners warming up for the first stade race was a youth named Coroebus from the king's own community, Elis. Hardly more than twenty years old, Coroebus was not very tall. His body was well proportioned, slim waisted, and broad shouldered; his legs were long and his chest deep. His entire body glistened under the fine film of oil that had been rubbed over his skin to protect it from sun rays and dust. Coroebus was barefooted. Around his waist he wore a loose, soft leather girdle. Coreobus was the ideal figure of a Greek athlete.

Coroebus and his rivals in the first Olympiad probably had to start from a simple line drawn in the earth. One day the starting line for the stade race would be a stone sill, fitted with two grooves for the runners' feet. This would be an advantage for future sprinters. They would press their feet against the grooves and grip the front rim with their bare toes.

At their starting positions, the first Olympic sprinters tensed their bodies, leaning forward with their arms extended, their heels raised. Each runner believed that a victory was the accomplishment of his god. Years later a winning runner would set up a statue of himself in Olympia, its base engraved with the legend "I belong to Zeus!"

The spectators at the first Olympiad fell suddenly silent as the voice of the herald rang out, warning the racers to get ready. A trumpeter raised his horn to his lips and the stade race was on!

Coroebus sprang forward, running with all the speed at his command. The other runners were closely bunched up beside him. Youthful arms flashed in the sunlight as the runners stretched every muscle. One hundred feet! Four hundred! And

*Runner at the starting line.
Bronze statuette,
fifth century B.C.*

Olympia Museum, photo N.A. Tombazi

65

a breathless, gasping finish at the end of the stadium! Coroebus was the winner. He trotted slowly to the judge's chair, in which the Elean king was sitting. King Iphitus wrapped Coroebus in his purple cloak, while the men of Elis cheered. At the altar in the sacred grove, the king presented the first Olympic stade-race victor with his reward—a crimson apple.

For the next three Olympiads, however, Elis could not produce a winning runner to follow in the footsteps of Coroebus. Winners in two successive Olympics came from Messenia, the rich city surrounded by fertile orchards, olive groves, and vineyards. King Iphitus, by now an old man, rejoiced as he awarded the victor's apple to his countryman in the fifth Olympiad.

But, as years passed, the aging king was troubled about the reward, since a red apple was not associated with the legends of Hercules and Olympia. So, for the seventh Olympiad, King Iphitus went back to consult the Oracle of Delphi. There the priestess told him to search for a "wild and fertile" olive tree, which he would find sheathed in a gossamer web. Back at Olympia, the king came upon a wild olive tree covered with cobwebs, shining with dew, growing in the *altis* in the midst of a green grove.

The wild olive tree was sacred to Olympia. According to Greek legend, it was first brought to the *altis* by Hercules from the land "at the back of the cold north wind," where a happy people called Hyperboreans were said to live in everlasting peace and sunshine. There, as the Greek poet Pindar describes Hercules' visit in his *Olympian Ode III*, the hero for the first time saw wild olive trees. He admired them and asked to be allowed to bring one back to Olympia. The gods of the Hyperboreans made a gift of an olive tree to Hercules, who planted it in the *altis* at Olympia.

He stood in wonder at the olive trees; he'd searched
so loyally for this, a plant whose leaves
would offer shade to all, and weave
a crown for excellence.

When King Iphitus came upon an olive tree in the *altis*, glistening in the morning sunlight, he ordered a fence set up around it and turned the spot into a shrine. Wreaths for the winners of the Olympic Games from that time on were to come from the branches of the sacred olive tree, each cut with a golden sickle by a young boy whose parents were both still living.

The wild olive is smaller than the cultivated tree. It has gray-green leaves and blossoms with fragrant white petals, but

*Harvesting olives.*
*Black-figured amphora,*
*sixth century* B.C.

British Museum

its fruit is not edible. A winner of an Olympic event received a wreath of wild olive branches and a headband of ram's wool.

Since the Olympic athlete contended for the honor of his city and the glory of the Olympian gods, the olive wreath and headband were the only tokens of victory he was supposed to expect. An Olympic athlete "belonged to Zeus," who was himself represented wearing a crown of wild olive boughs. When an athlete won an olive branch, he was believed to have joined the company of the gods. In time a victor could erect a statue in the holy grove at Olympia in celebration of his triumph, but officially the statue had to be only a symbol or representation. The statue could not be a likeness unless the athlete was a three-time winner.

King Iphitus surely hoped that the first wreath of olives would go to a runner from his own city of Elis. However, the aged king had to place the olive crown on the brow of an athlete from Messenia, named Daicles. From that seventh Olympiad in 752 B.C. until the eleventh, all winners of the Olympic stade race were from Messenia. But, when Messenia was destroyed by Sparta, its name disappeared from the list of Olympic winners. The olive crowns went to winners from other Greek cities, on the mainland or overseas.

Several hundred years later, the winner of the stade races staged in 416 B.C. and 412 B.C. was a young man, from Acragas in Sicily, named Exaenetus. When Exaenetus returned home from his second victory, he was escorted into the city in triumph by 300 horse-drawn chariots. According to one account, since an Olympic winner took on part of the identity of the gods, the walls of the city were breached to provide him with his own private entrance.

One outstanding athlete, Astylus, who won two races in 488 B.C., was unfaithful to his fellow citizens of Croton. In honor of his victories, his fellow Crotonites had erected a statue of him and given him a house to live in. But four years later Astylus appeared at Olympia claiming to be a Syracusan, in order, it was said angrily, to ingratiate himself with Gelon, the tyrant of the Sicilian city. Astylus won two events in the Olympic Games, and the people of Croton were so incensed that they pulled down his statue and converted his house into a prison.

An Olympic victory by one of its athletes was cause for rejoicing in every Greek community. Winning the classic stade race was especially desirable.

## DOUBLE STADE RACE (*Diaulos*)

The growing interest in the Games during the first half century of the historic Olympics made it necessary to add to the program of events. For the 14th Olympiad, in 724 B.C., a new foot race was scheduled—the *diaulos*, meaning the double flute. Its name described the race: twice the length of the stadium, a distance of 1,200 feet.

A young man from Corinth, named Dasmon, had won the classic stade race. There was rejoicing among the Corinthians as Dasmon received the olive crown for his victory. But the king of Elis seemed crestfallen. Fifty-two years had elapsed since his ancestor, King Iphitus, had revived the Games and thirty-six years since a winner had come from his own city-state of Elis. With the new event of the day, the double stade race, still to be run, maybe there would be yet another chance for an Elean runner.

Dasmon, the new stade race champion, was eager to become the first double winner at Olympia. He joined the other runners near the starting line and warmed up for the longer race. Among the contestants was a youth from Elis who seemed to avoid the young Pisatan runner waiting nearby. Despite years of quiet, the two communities could not forget the bitterness between them.

With the other runners, they practiced flying starts. Centuries later competitors in the *diaulos* would be going through the same motions. They took positions on the starting sill, their knees slightly bent, their bodies leaning forward, their right arms stretched in front to keep their balance. Each runner listened carefully for the signal so that he would start the race fairly and cleanly. No one wanted to be disqualified, or worse, beaten with long, forked branches by the officials in full view of the crowds.

The contestants stood at the starting end of the sandy track. At the far end of the track, 600 feet away, the posts for the stade race had been taken down. Only a central post remained, around which the runners would have to turn for the second, final lap to the finish. Getting around that post with the fewest possible steps was vitally important to the runners.

At the signal—a ringing blast of the trumpet—the contestants lunged forward and began racing at top speed toward the turning post. Every effort was strained to get an inside path around the post.

As the runners flew, the girdles around their waists clung to their bodies. Their arms and shoulders shone under a coating of oil, their hearts beat against their chests, and their lungs heaved. As they reached the central post, they edged one another, trying for the favored, inside position.

Dasmon reached the end of the forward stretch before all the other runners. But, as he moved to make his turn around the post, he found himself forced away from the inner path. He had to take an extra few steps to come around, and when he did, he saw two rivals ahead of him. Bare feet flew over the sand toward the finish line, while the onlookers screamed with excitement. First to touch the winning post was the runner from Pisa, the youthful Hypenus.

Soon Hypenus was standing before the throne of the king of Elis to receive his victor's crown. A smile of pride flickered on his lips, but the king could hardly hide his disappointment. Behind the king and the Pisatan victor, the waters of the sacred Alpheus River sparkled in the sunlight. The king arose from his chair to set the olive crown on Hypenus' forehead. Then, impulsively he threw his purple cloak over the shoulders of the glowing athlete and embraced him as though he were really one of his own countrymen from Elis.

Hypenus drew back from the king's arms and said he had to go back to his father and then home—to Pisa!

Nevertheless, many years later, the record of the 14th Olympiad was changed to list Hypenus as a champion from Elis.

# UPRIGHT WRESTLING

When the foot races were over, the crowds moved back into the *altis* for the exciting heavy events—wrestling, boxing, and the *pankration*. These events were staged in the open space before the Altar of Zeus.

Wrestling was probably the most popular athletic event in ancient Greece. The sport was considered a science and an art, the triumph of reason over barbarism and brute strength. Grace and skill were all-important. An opponent had not only to be thrown but thrown correctly and in good style. Wrestling was an essential part of the education of Greek boys, who spent much of their time in wrestling schools called *palaestrae*.

The fine points of the sport had been known for millennia, as early as 2,000 years before, by the first Pharaohs of Egypt. In Greece the hero Theseus was said to have learned the rules of wrestling from the goddess Athena. Vase paintings often depicted Hercules wrestling with giants and monsters.

There were two kinds of wrestling competitions in ancient Greece—upright and ground. In upright wrestling, the object was to throw one's opponent to the earth. In ground wrestling, hitting and kicking were allowed, and the struggle continued until one of the contestants acknowledged defeat. Ground wrestling was part of the *pankration*, which would take place later in the afternoon of the fourth day. Upright wrestling was a separate Olympic event as well as one of the five events comprising the *pentathlon*.

Unlike modern wrestling in which a throw is counted only when both shoulders of an opponent, or one shoulder and one hip, are made to touch the ground at the same time, a fair fall in ancient Greek upright wrestling was scored if one wrestler touched the ground with both knees or fell on any part of his body—his hips, back, or shoulders. The judges had the last word in deciding what constituted a clean throw.

*Wrestlers and trainer. Relief on pedestal of statue, sixth century B.C.*

National Museum, Athens, photo N.A. Tombazi

The rules of upright wrestling seem to have been:

1. Three clean falls are necessary for victory.
2. If both wrestlers fall to the ground, no score is counted.
3. Holds on all parts of the body are permitted.
4. Tripping is not penalized.
5. A fall on one knee is allowable for the "hoisting high" throw (now known as the "flying mare").
6. There is to be no struggling on the ground; no painful blows; no throttling an opponent; no twisting fingers, toes, arms, or legs to force an opponent to submit.

The athletes trained long and hard to master many intricate holds and throws. Every offensive hold had a defensive response. Even though tripping was allowed, it was considered wiser to reserve it for defense. Leg holds were rare because they could be dangerous; if the hold on an opponent's leg slipped, the athlete's own chances of being thrown increased greatly.

Once the rules were officially proclaimed, lots were drawn from a silver urn. The luck of the draw could make considerable difference in a wrestling competition. Many athletes, hoping for an advantage, set great store in magic charms, incanta-

*Sacrifice to the gods. Red-figured wine cup, sixth century B.C.*

Musée du Louvre, clichés des Musées Nationaux

tions, and prayers. If there was an odd number of contestants, one lucky athlete would win the first round without even competing; this was called a "dustless" victory because it was a victory without a struggle in the *skamma*, or sand pit.

The wrestling matches had been introduced into the Olympic program for the 18th Olympiad, staged in 708 B.C., the same year that the *pentathlon* was held for the first time. That year a Spartan named Eurybatus seemed favored to win the upright wrestling competition. Eurybatus was big, with powerful limbs and bulging muscles.

Eurybatus battered his way through the first round. Then he went on to overcome his second-round opponent, who had won his opening match "without dust" and thus had the advantage of being fully rested. Finally only two wrestlers remained for the deciding bout. Eurybatus faced the remaining finalist. He turned to his adversary, his feet planted firmly in the loose sand of the *skamma*, a stance designed to give his opponent no opening. Meanwhile he searched for an opportunity with outstretched hands. The two circled one another, reaching, retreating, looking for an opening. Sometimes the wrestlers leaned against one another, butting their heads like rams in battle. Then again they rested their heads on one another's shoulders, or turned their bodies sideways to force a false move.

A wrestler might hold his opponent's wrists to prevent him from getting a neck or body hold. In one spectacular wrestling maneuver, the "hoisting high," a wrestler would seize his opponent's arms at the wrist and elbow, and then, rapidly turning his own back, use the arms as a lever to hoist the rival over his head. To complete the throw, the wrestler stepped forward or even sank to one knee.

The wrestlers in the final round of the first Olympic match watched each other's slightest movements for the possibility of

*Wrestlers practicing "flying mare." Red-figured vase, fifth century B.C.*

British Museum

a throw. It was not easy for the spectators to distinguish between the two naked men circling around on the soft sand, reaching for a hold on the hand, the body, or the neck. With a flurry of motion, a body fell. Then again, a third time, and a fourth. The score was tied—two throws scored by each wrestler.

With a flash of movement, one of the young men was thrown to the ground, his body pinned firmly on the sand. The winner stood up—it was Eurybatus.

Perhaps the most celebrated of all Olympic wrestlers was Milo of Croton, a town in southern Italy. Croton was famous for its healthful climate, its medical academy, and its school of philosophy. Milo won his first Olympic victory as a boy in the 60th Olympiad, 540 B.C. Eight years later he won the men's event and went on to repeat his triumphs in the next five

Olympiads. His fame as a wrestler was so great that at one Olympiad no one dared oppose him.

Milo was finally defeated by a younger opponent, Timasitheus, who also came from Croton. Timasitheus evaded all Milo's wrestling holds and wore him out so, the aging wrestler finally had to give up.

In addition to his victories at Olympia, Milo won six times in the Pythian Games at Delphi, ten times at Isthmia, and nine times in the Nemean Games. Milo's great strength was celebrated, as was his prodigious appetite. He carried his own heavy statue into the *altis* and set it up himself to celebrate his victories. On one occasion he held a pomegranate in his hand and defied anyone to force him to release it. Many tried but no one succeeded. To everyone's amazement, when Milo relaxed his grip, the fruit was revealed uncrushed, with no sign of a blemish. Milo was credited with having such controlled strength that he could tie a headband of wool around his forehead and snap it by expanding the blood vessels under his skin. Once he picked up a four-year-old bull, slung it across his shoulders, and paraded around the stadium at Olympia to the immense delight of all the spectators. He then had the bull butchered and proceeded to eat it all in a single day.

Tales of Milo's strength spread throughout the Greek-speaking world and reached even the ears of Darius, the king of Persia. One well-known story of his physical prowess told of a time when the pillar in the room in which Milo was dining began to shake, as if an earthquake were convulsing the city. Milo single-handedly supported the pillar, holding up the ceiling while the other guests managed to get out of the room and save their lives. Afterward he somehow succeeded in escaping himself.

Milo met his death by relying too much on his brute strength. One day he was walking in the countryside near

Croton, when by chance he came upon a withered tree into which wedges had been driven in order to split the trunk. Milo, thinking that he would finish the job himself, put his hands and feet into the cleft in the tree trunk and tried to pull the trunk apart by his own strength. Unfortunately the wedges slipped out and the tree trunk sprang back together, holding him in an unbreakable grip. He was a prisoner of the old tree, an easy prey for the wild wolves which roamed the area in great numbers.

Years after his death, memories of Milo lingered at Olympia. Even a century later, as the crowds watched the wrestlers compete with the graceful ease of dancers, the thought still persisted that no Olympic wrestler had ever appeared who could be compared to him.

# BOXING

After the wrestling match was over, the crowds stayed on to watch the Olympic boxers in action. Boxing had been added to the program of events for the 23rd Olympiad in 688 B.C. That year the number of Festival days had been expanded to accommodate the growing roster of games.

Greek boxers were not classified according to weight, so big men had a decided advantage. There was no boxing ring; instead, the bout was fought in an open space. The boxer's target was the head and face of his opponent rather than the body. Holding was not allowed, and blows could be parried with the flat of the hand.

Boxers' hands were bound with long thongs of leather and

*Boxers with trainer before match. Red-figured amphora, fifth century* B.C.

the fingers were left free. Soft leather straps were wrapped around the upper part of the palm so that the boxer could clench his fist for a punch.

Boxing matches did not have rounds, and the fighters had no rest periods. A boxer was allowed to pause momentarily to catch his breath, but the rule was that the fight had to go on to a conclusion, until one of the boxers was knocked out or could no longer defend himself. A boxer could acknowledge defeat and end the battle at any time by holding up his index finger or by pointing two fingers at his opponent. Boxing was one of the few sports in which victory could depend on the surrender of one of the contestants. The Spartans objected to this rule. Spartans did not mind losing a contest, but they were against anything involving the idea of surrender, because giving up was against all of their ideals and training. For this reason Spartans rarely competed in the boxing matches.

In ancient Olympic boxing matches there was no rule against hitting an opponent when he was down. As a result, the fighters moved slowly and cautiously, preferring to stay on the defensive rather than risk the danger of the offensive. The bouts were often so long and tedious that spectators would drift away.

If the judges felt the fight was going on too long, they could order a "climax." Then the combatants exchanged blows one at a time without attempting to defend themselves. Alternately they struck one another until one yielded. The "climax," like the boxing match itself, in time became bloody and brutal. Soft leather thongs, the first boxing gloves, were replaced by straps of hard, tanned ox hide. Rings and other objects with sharp edges were attached to the gloves, with the result that boxers had their teeth broken, their noses smashed, and their eyes and ears battered. Serious injury was common, and accidental deaths inevitable. If one of the boxers was killed, the dead man was immediately awarded the victor's crown.

Among the competitors who presented themselves for the first Olympic boxing match was Onomastus of Smyrna, a city in Asia Minor. Onomastus became the winner of the first boxing competition in an Olympic Game, and his victory was the first triumph for a Greek city off the mainland.

Because of the advantage of size, boxing became more and more the domain of big men with powerful physiques. These huge men, in time, came to regard the sport as a profession, a way to win prizes and prize money. The competitors were no longer the wealthy sons of noble Greek families, to whom victory was a matter of family and civic pride.

One boxer who was surrounded by legend was Glaucus of Carystus. One day he was plowing a field for his father, Demy-

lus, when the plowshare broke off. Demylus found his son hammering the plowshare blade back in place with his bare fists. His son's strength so impressed the old man that he decided to take him to Olympia to compete in the boxing competition. In spite of the fact that he was completely untrained, young Glaucus by sheer strength fought his way to the finals, although he suffered a bloody battering in the process. When it looked as if the badly wounded Glaucus would have to yield, his father shouted to him over the roar of the spectators: "Remember the plowshare!" Glaucus heard his father's voice, turned, and hit his opponent so hard that the contest came to an immediate end.

Perhaps the most famous of all Olympic boxing champions was Diagoras of Rhodes, who won the boxing bout in the 79th Olympiad in 464 B.C. He was the father of a family of Olympic champions. In the 83rd Olympiad in 448 B.C., Diagoras' two elder sons won laurel wreaths in the same Games. Damagetus, the eldest, won the *pankration*, repeating his victory of the previous Olympiad, while Acusilaus, the second son, won the boxing match. The two brothers lifted their aged father onto their shoulders, and the three Olympic champions paraded around the *altis.* Years later Diagoras' youngest son, Dorieus, won the *pankration* in three successive Olympiads— the 87th, 88th, and 89th, staged in 432 B.C., 428 B.C. and 424 B.C.

Diagoras' fame hung over the *altis.* The achievements of his family never seemed to cease. His nephew Eucles won the boxing match in 404 B.C., in the 94th Olympiad, the same Olympiad in which Diagoras' grandson Pisirodus won the boys' boxing event.

*Boxers. Black-figured amphora, fourth century B.C.*

# THE *PANKRATION*

The *pankration*, a combination of both wrestling and boxing, was usually the last of the heavy events following the foot races on the fourth day. The name of the event meant all-powerful or all-strong.

Pancratiasts used every part of their bodies—hands, feet, elbows, knees, necks, and even their heads. Competitors tried everything. They bit each other and tried to gouge out one another's eyes, to dislocate opponents' fingers or arms, and to get strangleholds around the neck.

Pancratiasts were trained never to show fear. If one had taken enough punishment and wished to submit, he raised his hand. As in boxing, the possibility of having to admit defeat kept Spartans from competing in the event.

Sometimes the *pankration* was so savage that a contestant lost his life. In 564 B.C., Arrhichion of Phigalia, winner of two previous *pankration* crowns at Olympia, died after his adversary trapped him in a combined leg- and stranglehold. Even though Arrhichion, trying to escape, had dislocated his opponent's ankle, the stranglehold proved fatal. The dead man was immediately proclaimed the victor of the match.

Because the *pankration* was the most savage of all the events in the Olympic program, it was extremely popular with the spectators. In A.D. 25, at the 201st Olympiad, Sarapion of Alexandria was fined for cowardice. He ran away before his bout because he was afraid of his opponents. In 480 B.C., at the 75th Olympiad, Theagenes of Thasos, who claimed descent from Hercules, disappointed the crowds when he withdrew from the *pankration* because he had tired himself out winning the boxing match. Theagenes was nevertheless one of the most

*Pancratiasts and trainer. Black-figured amphora, fifth century B.C.*

popular athletes in ancient Greek games. With his great strength, he won 1,400 victories in various athletic festivals during his lifetime. Even as a child he had been big and strong like Hercules. He was only nine years old when he picked up a heavy bronze statue of his hero and carried it home from the market place in Thasos.

To celebrate Theagenes' victories, statues of him were set up around the city of Thasos for his fellow citizens to admire. But one defeated adversary could not get over his disgrace even after Theagenes died. The defeated athlete began to flog one of the statues of Theagenes in the city square, as if to avenge

*Pancratiasts. Red-figured bowl, fifth century* B.C.

himself. One night the statue toppled over and crushed the frustrated athlete to death. The dead man's children raised a cry that their father's death had to be atoned for and that the statue should be charged with murder. Strangely enough, the statue was put on trial, found guilty, and condemned. The court ordered it to be thrown into the sea.

From that moment on, calamity overtook the land of Thasos. The rains stopped falling and the crops withered in the scorching heat. In despair, the Thasians turned to the Oracle of Delphi for advice. They were told to bring home everyone who had been exiled. Despite the difficulties of the undertaking, they called back home all of their people who had been sent away. The land nevertheless continued barren and unfruitful. The oracle reminded the Thasians that they had forgotten Theagenes at the bottom of the sea. What were they to do? The Thasians continued to suffer until the day the bronze statue was caught in a fisherman's net. It was quickly restored to its place in Thasos, where Theagenes came to be worshiped as an immortal, and the land was soon blooming again.

Another powerful pancratiast renowned for his enormous strength was Polydamas of Scotussa. He reportedly killed a lion with his bare hands and stopped a racing chariot by seizing it with one hand. According to legend, Polydamas was in a mountain cave with some friends when suddenly the ceiling began crumbling over their heads. His friends fled to safety outside the cave but Polydamas refused to leave. He tried to hold up the falling ceiling of the cave, refusing to admit that the mountain over his head was more powerful than he was. And so he was crushed to death when the ceiling caved in.

In every Olympic Festival, big, lumbering men came forward, ready to endure the most painful punishments in order to win a coveted crown of wild olive branches. Even as the afternoon sun of the fourth day of the Olympiad sank slowly toward the western horizon, the pancratiasts struggled, trying their utmost to force their opponents to submit. Pancratiasts were huge, powerful men, but few could compare to the Herculean figures of Theagenes or Polydamas.

# RACE IN ARMOR (*Hoplite* Race)

By late afternoon of the fourth day of the Olympics, the spectators had their fill of running, wrestling, boxing, and the savage *pankration*. But there was still one last event to come —the *hoplite* race, the race in armor.

This final competition was both serious and comic. It was

Hoplite *racer. Red-figured vase, fifth century* B.C.

a race of 1,200 feet, twice the length of the stadium, for men in armor. This race had been run for the first time in the 65th Olympiad in 520 B.C. The competitors were not necessarily athletes but were usually soldiers, who lent the Festival a military character. The race dramatized the need for military training in Greece in the face of the menacing growth of the Persian Empire in Asia. In the year 546–545 B.C., King Cyrus of Persia had taken control of all the Greek communities in Asia Minor.

The runners in the *hoplite* race wore heavy pieces of armor, plumed helmets, weighty greaves, or leg guards, and carried round shields. They did not carry swords or spears lest they harm an opponent in the excitement of the race.

The first winner was Demaratus, a soldier from Heraea. Four years later he returned to the 66th Olympiad to win the *hoplite* race a second time. Demaratus became the father of a whole family of Olympic champions. His son, Theopompus, won the *pentathlon* in the 74th and 75th Olympiads. His grandson, also named Theopompus, was a wrestling champion who won two successive victories in 440 B.C. and 436 B.C.

By that time the threat of Persian domination had diminished. In 490 B.C. a battle was fought at Marathon, and the Persians were defeated. After forty more years of warfare, a peace had been concluded in 449 B.C. Consequently, the strict military air of the *hoplite* race faded. The spectacle of men lumbering along in heavy costumes of metal became a source of delight and amusement to the crowds. The heavier pieces of armor were eventually discarded to let the runners get up a little speed.

The *hoplite* race was not really an athletic event. Its appeal was to the citizen soldier, not the specialized athlete. This race certainly must have been a reminder that the peace of the sacred truce would soon be over and that the quiet of the Olympic Games would be followed by bitter armed struggle, so typical of Greek history.

The crowds in the stadium at Olympia kept thinning out as the afternoon waned. The onlookers, watching the last event of the Festival, the *hoplite* race, were laughing and cheering. It had been an exciting Olympiad, filled with suspense, triumph, and despair. It was time to think of getting ready for the hard journey home.

# THE FIFTH DAY:
## *The Victory Banquet*

NO ATHLETIC EVENTS were scheduled for the fifth and last day of the Olympic Festival. In the morning another procession wound through the *altis* toward the Temple of Zeus, while the entire Olympic community looked on. Marching in the procession were the judges, the members of visiting delegations, and the proud young champions, whom everyone strained to see. Each Olympic victor carried in his right hand a palm branch, awarded him after the judges made their decision and the heralds proclaimed his name. The palm branch was considered a symbol of victory because it was resilient and did not buckle or flatten under pressure.

Standing in the magnificent Temple of Zeus, before Phidias' awesome gold-and-ivory statue of the king of the gods, each winning athlete exchanged his palm branch for the cherished crown of wild olives. Even the great figure of Zeus was crowned with a gold wreath of wild olives, to commemorate his victory over the old gods at Olympia. And as the judges placed a wreath on the victor's head, each victor became linked with the gods. Outside the temple, the spectators showered the newly crowned champions with flowers and leaves.

There was little left for the visitors at Olympia to do but to gather up their belongings for the long trip home. Booths and tents were taken down. Horses, mules, and carriages were

*Boxers practicing to flute music. Black-figured jar, sixth century B.C.*

hired. Provisions were bought for the journey. Only the defeated stole away with as little attention as possible.

*Tired athlete.*
*Red-figured wine cup,*
*fifth century B.C.*

Virginia Museum of Fine Arts, Richmond.
Purchase 1962, The Williams Fund Income

The poet Pindar described the retreat of unsuccessful boy athletes in his *Pythian Ode VIII*:

> For the losers, no laughter,
> no gay home-coming was given.
> They went back to their mothers
> without delight, creeping
> through narrow alleys, and avoiding
> the other contestants. They felt
> the hurt of failure.

90

There was great rejoicing among the contingents from city-states that had produced a champion. In 392 B.C. a young lad named Dicon from the community of Caulonia, near Syracuse, won the boys' stade race. The ruler of Syracuse tried to bribe the boy's father to proclaim him a Syracusan, but Dicon's father refused. By 384 B.C. his home community had been destroyed, so for the 99th Olympiad, Dicon ran as a Syracusan and won. In addition to winning three olive crowns at Olympia, Dicon also won five times in the Pythian Games, staged at Delphi in honor of Apollo; three times in the Isthmian Games near Corinth, where athletic contests were held in honor of Poseidon, god of the sea; and four times in the Nemean Games, where the festival honored Zeus. The prize for winning was a laurel wreath at Delphi, a pine wreath at Isthmia, and a wreath of wild celery at Nemea.

Many of the athletes, however, were beginning to seek richer prizes than victors' crowns of olive, laurel, pine, or wild celery. Sport was becoming more and more professional, a way for talented young men of low station to amass wealth and to make their way upward in the ancient Greek world. And with professionalism came corruption, cheating, and attempts to bribe. In the 96th Olympiad, held in 396 B.C., the stade race, according to two of the three judges, had been won by Eupolemus of Elis. The third judge disagreed, favoring Leon of Ambracia as the victor. The victory of Eupolemus was appealed to the sponsors of the Games in Elis, with athletes from Crete and Corinth joining the protest. The council in Elis upheld the appeal of the protesting runner and ordered the two judges punished. But the award, once given, could not be rescinded.

Eight years later bribery was uncovered in the boxing matches. Eupolus of Thessaly, it was discovered, had bribed his opponents to let him win. One of the boxers who took the bribe was Phormio of Halicarnassus, an Olympic champion himself, who had won the event four years before. Heavy fines were imposed by the Elean sponsors of the Games. These fines were used to make six bronze statues of Zeus, which were set up at the entrance to the stadium as warnings to the competitors. The statues were called *zanes*. They were inscribed: "Not with money, but with speed of foot and strength of body must prizes be won at Olympia."

Some fifty years later, in the 112th Olympiad, held in 332 B.C., Callipus of Athens was found guilty of bribing his opponents in the *pentathlon* to let him win. Again Elis imposed a heavy fine on the athlete's community, but Athens refused to pay. The city-state soon found out, however, that the Oracle of Delphi was ignoring all pleas for advice from Athenians until the fine was paid. The money was thereupon handed over. Six more statues of Zeus were erected in the row leading to the entrance to the stadium.

But not only did the Hellanodicae of Elis punish bribery, the offending athlete's own countrymen frowned on the practice. In the 99th Olympiad, the long-distance *dolichos* was won by Sotades from the island of Crete. Four years later Sotades returned to Olympia and entered the long-distance race under the banner of the city-state of Ephesus. Sotades was accused of having accepted a bribe to change, and when he won, his countrymen banished him from Crete.

For the victors who had won their olive crowns fairly, there was rejoicing for the remainder of the Festival. As they received their crowns, they sang, "Hail Lord Hercules, lovely in victory." The winning athletes were surrounded by friends, who sang and danced to the accompaniment of a flute or lyre. Such a celebration is described in Pindar's *Pythian Ode I*:

O golden lyre, Apollo and the dark-haired
muses share your power. Singers' voices
    and the gay feet of dancers
    obey you, when your vibrating
strings begin the Chorus-Song.

Gold instrument, your music calms
the angry thunder-flash, and listening,
    the eagle, lord of air,
    folding his rapid wings,
sleeps on the staff of Zeus.

The joy of the trainers, parents, brothers, and companions
was unrestrained for the "son [who had] put on his young hair
the wings of glory for Games won." Everyone would sing.
Pindar's *Olympian Ode VIII* praises the winners:

Mistress of gold-crowned Festivals,
Olympia, Lady of Truth—your priests
with ceremony and with sacrifice
call on Lord Zeus:

"Bright Thunderer, what Word have you
for those competing here? Their hearts
seek praise for high accomplishment
    and rest from pain."

    Truly, Zeus sends to men
    who honor him, the grace
    of answered prayer.

O Olympian grove, made lovely
with river and well-growing trees,

welcome this Victory Song,
welcome your garlanded winner!

Whoever wins your shining
prize, Olympia,
wears glory always.


The final event of the Festival was a great banquet for all the victorious athletes, given by the Hellanodicae of Elis. The main course was the meat of the hundred animals sacrificed to Zeus on the third day of the Games. The banquet went on for hours, while songs of triumph resounded through the Prytaneum. The feasters consumed mountains of meat and drank the fresh wine from nearby vineyards.

All the while, they paid homage to their gods in song. Pindar's *Olympian Ode X* echoes the festive spirit:

The packed crowd gave
a great cheer. The moon's clear face
lit up the evening, and the holy place
overflowed with feasting
and holiday song.


Night had descended over the Alpheus valley. The moon was high over the hills. In the morning the athletes would turn their steps again toward home. At the end of their journeys they would be back once more with their families and friends. The people of their city-states would receive them in triumph. With more dancing and singing, the victorious athletes would be escorted to their temples, where they would dedicate to their own god or hero the olive crowns of victory which they had brought back from Olympia. Pindar's *Olympian Ode II* connects the victors to the gods:

*Celebrating victory. Black-figured jar, sixth century* B.C.

O songs that rule my lyre—
what god, what hero,
what man shall we sing of?

Truly, Zeus is god
of Olympia; the hero
Hercules began these Games,
spending gold he'd seized in war—

but now we shall celebrate a winner!
He drove his four-horse
chariot to victory.

95

# THE END OF THE
# ANCIENT GAMES

GREECE LOST ITS freedom when it was made part of a Roman province in 146 B.C. The Olympic Games, however, went on without interruption, despite one attempt to move them to Rome. Roman aristocrats and athletes now came across the seas to compete with Greek athletes in the ancient Games. For a while, though, the splendor that had marked the Festival seems to have faded.

When Augustus Caesar became the Emperor of Rome in 31 B.C., he ordered all wars within the Empire to cease. This *pax Romana*, or Roman peace, helped revive the popularity of the ancient Games.

In A.D. 37, the year that Emperor Tiberius died, a boy named Nero was born in Rome. He was destined to rule the Roman world. As Emperor, Nero considered himself not only a statesman but also a poet, musician, actor, and athlete. He decided that competition in the arts should be added to the Olympic Festival.

He wanted to participate in the Games in person, but he could not arrange to get to Olympia for the regular Olympiad scheduled for A.D. 65. At his command the 211th Festival was postponed.

When it was held, two years later, Emperor Nero appeared in a contest for tragedians and a contest for singers, accompanying himself on a zither. He was the only person who took part in those contests and was awarded an olive crown for each competition. Nero also entered the chariot race—with a team of ten horses. He handled the reins himself. As the carriage careened around the racecourse, the pudgy Roman ruler was thrown to the ground. All competing chariots halted while attendants rushed to help Nero remount his chariot. He was too tired to finish the race, so he handed the reins to a driver. He was nevertheless declared the winner and awarded a third olive crown. A year later, however, Nero was dead, and the whole 211th Festival was declared invalid. The gifts which Nero had showered on the Greeks were recalled by the Emperor Vespasian. The new Emperor re-imposed the taxes on the Peloponnesus that Nero had forgiven, and re-established Roman rule, which Nero had relaxed. The reason for the harsh Roman action, the Emperor said, was that the Greeks no longer knew the meaning of liberty.

A century later, interest in Greece was revived in Rome. During the rule of Emperor Hadrian (A.D. 117–138), the Olympic Festival regained some of its importance. At this time many contemporary accounts of the Festival were written by Roman historians and travelers, particularly by the chronicler Pausanias of Lydia, who visited Olympia in A.D. 174. It was then that the stadium at Olympia was rebuilt for the last time.

The Olympic Games continued every fourth year for the following two centuries. Around A.D. 312, Emperor Constantine the Great accepted Christianity and proclaimed it as the faith of the Roman Empire. In A.D. 391 all pre-Christian cults were banned by Emperor Theodosius I, and Zeus the thunderer and all the other gods of Mount Olympus were banished. The last Olympiad, the 293rd, was probably held in A.D. 393. It ended a tradition that had lasted for 1,168 years. Other accounts say that the Olympic Festivals continued until after the

Temple of Zeus burned down in a fire in the *altis* in A.D. 426. The fire may have been set on the orders of Theodosius II, who ruled the eastern part of the Roman Empire from A.D. 408 to A.D. 450.

About thirty years before the Temple of Zeus burned down, the great statue of the god by Phidias had been removed to Constantinople. Unfortunately, the statue was destroyed when the palace in which it was set up was consumed by a fire that razed much of Constantinople in A.D. 462.

With the Festival now abandoned, the sacred *altis*, the olive groves, and the plane trees were returned to the wind and the rain. Wandering tribesmen, the Goths, the Visigoths, and the Slavs, came to Olympia looking for booty. No one cared for the sacred grounds, and the rains, pouring down the hillsides of the Hill of Cronus, soon washed away the racecourse and parts of the stadium. In time the Cladeus River broke out of the dam that held its wild waters in check and covered the grove with layers of mud. Earthquakes devastated the sanctuary and toppled the pillars of the temples. The mighty Alpheus changed its course and covered the ruins with mud. Nothing was left to mark the site where 40,000 Greeks once stood in the sun, cheering on the contestants in the Olympic Games.

Zeus. *Bronze,*
*sixth century B.C.*

National Museum, Athens,
photo N.A. Tombazi

99

# THE MODERN
# OLYMPICS

OLYMPIA LAY BURIED in mud for about 1,400 years. Early in the nineteenth century, archaeologists began to explore the remains of the Temple of Zeus, and they have been digging in the area ever since.

A French nobleman, Baron Pierre de Coubertin, envisioned a modern revival of the ancient Games, and he spent many years appealing for support from the nations of the world. In 1896 he finally was able to restage the Games for the first time in fourteen centuries. Now every four years a "priestess" lights an Olympic flame from the light of the sun, enters the stadium in Olympia, and hands the torch to a priestly "king" of the new Olympiad. He passes the torch to the leader of a team of runners, who usher it out of the *altis* to a grove dedicated to Baron de Coubertin. There an urn is lit on a modern altar, where it burns for the entire duration of the Games.

Another torch, lit from the urn on the altar, is carried by relays of runners until the Olympic flame has reached a temporary home, wherever in the world the Games are about to take place.

*The* palaestra *at Olympia as it looks today.*

photo N.A. Tombazi

100

# IMPORTANT DATES

*Jumper landing in the*
skamma. *Bronze statuette,*
*fifth century B.C.*

The Metropolitan Museum of Art,
Rogers Fund, 1908

# IMPORTANT DATES

| | |
|---|---|
| about 1050 – 950 B.C. | Greek colonization of Asia Minor. |
| about 1000 B.C. | Main invasion of the Peloponnesus by Dorian Greeks. |
| 776 B.C. | First historic Olympiad. Stade-race winner, Coroebus of Elis. |
| 752 B.C. | First awarding of olive wreath as Olympic prize. |
| about 750 B.C. | Greek colonization of Italy and Sicily. |
| about 735 –715 B.C. | Spartan conquest of Messenia. |
| 734 B.C. | Founding of Syracuse. |
| 724 B.C. | 14th Olympiad: new event, *diaulos* (double stade race), introduced. Winner, Hypenus of Pisa. |
| 721 B.C. | Founding of Sybaris. |
| 720 B.C. | Homer completes epic poem the *Iliad.* 15th Olympiad: new event, *dolichos* (long race), introduced. Winner, Acanthus of Sparta. |
| 710 –708 B.C. | Founding of Croton. |
| 708 B.C. | 18th Olympiad: new events, *pentathlon* and wrestling, introduced. *Pentathlon* winner, Lampis of Sparta. Wrestling winner, Eurybatus of Sparta. |
| 688 B.C. | Founding of Gela. 23rd Olympiad: new event, boxing, introduced. Winner, Onomastus of Smyrna. |
| 680 B.C. | 25th Olympiad: new event, chariot race with teams of four horses, introduced. Winner, Pagondas of Thebes. |

104

| | |
|---|---|
| about 669 B.C. | Pheidon, ruler of Argos, defeats Sparta. |
| about 650 B.C. | Messenian revolt crushed by Sparta. |
| 648 B.C. | 33rd Olympiad: new events, *pankration* and horse race, introduced. *Pankration* winner, Lygdamis of Syracuse. Horse-race winner, Crauxidas of Crannon. |
| 632 B.C. | 37th Olympiad: new events, boys' foot race and wrestling, introduced. Foot-race winner, Polynices of Sparta. Wrestling winner, Hipposthenes of Sparta. |
| 628 B.C. | 38th Olympiad: new event, boys' *pentathlon*, introduced. Winner, Eutelidas of Sparta. |
| 616 B.C. | 41st Olympiad: new event, boys' boxing, introduced. Winner, Philyatis of Sybaris. |
| about 570 B.C. | Eleans gain control of Olympic Games. |
| 540 B.C. | Milo of Croton wins first of seven Olympic crowns. |
| 525 – 456 B.C. | Lifetime of dramatist Aeschylus. |
| 522 – 442 B.C. | Lifetime of poet Pindar. |
| 520 B.C. | 65th Olympiad: new event, race in armor (*hoplite* race), introduced. Winner, Demaratus of Heraea. |
| 510 B.C. | Athens overthrows tyrant Pisistratus. |
| 500 B.C. | 70th Olympiad: new event, chariot race for mules, introduced. Winner, Thersos of Thessaly. |
| 496 B.C. | 71st Olympiad: new event, chariot race for mares, introduced. Winner, Pataicos of Dyma. |
| 490 B.C. | Battle of Marathon. Persians defeated by Greeks. |
| 484 – 430 B.C. | Lifetime of historian Herodotus. |
| 484 – 406 B.C. | Lifetime of dramatist Euripides. |

| | |
|---|---|
| 480 B.C. | Battle of Salamis. Persian fleet defeated by Greeks. |
| 476 – 472 B.C. | Pindar writes *Olympian Odes I, II*, and *III*. |
| about 470 B.C. | Birth of Greece's first great painter, Polygnotus. |
| 469 –399 B.C. | Lifetime of philosopher Socrates. |
| 464 B.C. | Diagoras of Rhodes wins first of four Olympic crowns. |
| 460 – 450 B.C. | Sculptor Myron creates *Discus Thrower*. |
| 460 – 370 B.C. | Lifetime of Hippocrates, "Father of Medicine." |
| 456 B.C. | Temple of Zeus at Olympia completed. |
| 454 B.C. | Pericles in control of Athens. |
| 450 – 430 B.C. | Polyclitus produces masterpieces of sculpture. |
| 450 –388 B.C. | Lifetime of dramatist Aristophanes. |
| 448 – 442 B.C. | Construction of the Parthenon in Athens. |
| 435 B.C. | Sculptor Phidias completes statue of Zeus in temple at Olympia. |
| 432 B.C. | Dorieus, son of Diagoras, wins first of three Olympic *pankration* crowns. |
| 431– 404 B.C. | Peloponnesian Wars. |
| 413– 406 B.C. | Dramatist Sophocles writes tragedies. |
| 408 B.C. | 93rd Olympiad: new event, chariot race for teams of two horses, introduced. Winner, Eugoras of Elis. |
| 399 B.C. | Sparta invades Elis. |
| 396 B.C. | 96th Olympiad: new events, contests for heralds and trumpeters, introduced. Winner of contest for heralds, Timaios of Elis. Winner of contest for trumpeters, Crater of Elis. |
| 388 B.C. | 98th Olympiad: new event, chariot race for teams of four colts, introduced. Winner, |

| | Eurybiades of Sparta. |
|---|---|
| 365–364 B.C. | Arcadians invade Elis and take temporary control of Olympia. |
| 359–336 B.C. | Reign of Philip II of Macedonia. |
| 350–330 B.C. | Sculptor Praxiteles creates masterpieces of sculpture. |
| 336–323 B.C. | Reign of Alexander the Great. Palm branch introduced as an immediate symbol of victory in Olympic Games. |
| about 300 B.C. | Euclid develops principles of geometry. |
| 287–212 B.C. | Lifetime of mathematician and scientist Archimedes. |
| 268 B.C. | 128th Olympiad: new event, chariot race for teams of two colts, introduced. |
| 256 B.C. | 131st Olympiad: new event, race for colts, introduced. |
| 200 B.C. | 145th Olympiad: new event, *pankration* for boys, introduced. |
| 146 B.C. | Greece becomes Roman province and named Achaea. |
| 106–44 B.C. | Lifetime of Cicero, Roman statesman and orator. |
| 100–44 B.C. | Lifetime of Julius Caesar. |
| 79–19 B.C. | Lifetime of Virgil, author of *The Aeneid*. |
| about 50 B.C. | First association of professional athletes formed. |
| 31 B.C. | Roman Empire founded. |
| 12 B.C. | Herod, king of Judea, presides over Olympic Games. |
| | |
| A.D. 14 | Death of Roman Emperor Augustus Caesar. |
| A.D. 68 | Death of Roman Emperor Nero. |

| | |
|---|---|
| A.D. 160–174 | Pausanias visits Olympia and writes about his travels. |
| A.D. 312 | Emperor Constantine the Great accepts Christianity as official faith of Roman Empire. |
| about A.D. 360 | Fire in Constantinople destroys Phidias' statue of Zeus. |
| A.D. 393 | 293rd Olympiad. Emperor Theodosius I abolishes Olympic Festival. |
| about A.D. 426 | Temple of Zeus at Olympia destroyed by fire. |
| A.D. 1829 | Archaeologists from France begin excavating Temple of Zeus. |
| A.D. 1875 | Ernst Curtius begins German archaeological expeditions, which are still digging at Olympia. |
| A.D. 1896 | First modern Olympiad staged in Athens, under direction of Baron de Coubertin. |
| A.D. 1900 | Olympic Games held in Paris. |
| A.D. 1904 | Olympic Games held in St. Louis, Missouri. |
| A.D. 1906 | Unofficial Olympic Games held in Athens. |
| A.D. 1908 | Olympic Games held in London. |
| A.D. 1912 | Olympic Games held in Stockholm. |
| A.D. 1916 | Olympic Games canceled. World War I. |
| A.D. 1920 | Olympic Games held in Antwerp. |
| A.D. 1924 | Olympic Games held in Paris. |
| A.D. 1928 | Olympic Games held in Amsterdam. |
| A.D. 1932 | Olympic Games held in Los Angeles. |
| A.D. 1936 | Olympic Games held in Berlin. |
| A.D. 1940–1944 | Olympic Games canceled. World War II. |
| A.D. 1948 | Olympic Games held in London. |
| A.D. 1952 | Olympic Games held in Helsinki. |
| A.D. 1956 | Olympic Games held in Melbourne. |
| A.D. 1960 | Olympic Games held in Rome. |

A.D. 1964    Olympic Games held in Tokyo.
A.D. 1968    Olympic Games held in Mexico City.
A.D. 1972    Olympic Games held in Munich.
A.D. 1976    Olympic Games held in Montreal.
A.D. 1980    Olympic Games held in Moscow.
A.D. 1984    Olympic Games held in Los Angeles.

# INDEX

*Roman coin with head
of Zeus, after statue
by Phidias, second century* A.D.

Staatliche Museen, East Berlin

# INDEX

Page numbers in italics refer to art.

# Other Books

## By SHIRLEY GLUBOK

Art and Archaeology

The Art of Africa

The Art of America from Jackson to Lincoln

The Art of America in the Early Twentieth Century

The Art of America in the Gilded Age

The Art of America Since World War II

The Art of Ancient Egypt

The Art of Ancient Greece

The Art of Ancient Mexico

The Art of Ancient Peru

The Art of Ancient Rome

The Art of China

The Art of Colonial America

The Art of India

The Art of Japan

The Art of Lands in the Bible

The Art of the Eskimo

The Art of the Etruscans

The Art of the New American Nation

The Art of the North American Indian

The Art of the Northwest Coast Indians

The Art of the Old West

The Art of the Plains Indians

The Art of the Southwest Indians

The Art of the Spanish in the United States and Puerto Rico

The Art of the Woodland Indians

The Fall of the Aztecs

The Fall of the Incas

Dolls Dolls Dolls

Digging in Assyria

Discovering the Royal Tombs at Ur

Discovering Tut-Ankh-Amen's Tomb

Home and Child Life in Colonial Days

Knights in Armor

## By ALFRED TAMARIN and SHIRLEY GLUBOK

Ancient Indians of the Southwest

Voyaging to Cathay: Americans in the China Trade

## By ALFRED TAMARIN

The Autobiography of Benvenuto Cellini

Benjamin Franklin: An Autobiographical Portrait

Fire Fighting in America

Japan and the United States: The Early Encounters

Revolt in Judea: The Road to Masada

We Have Not Vanished: Eastern Indians of the United States

Designed by Kohar Alexanian
Set in 12 pt. Times Roman
Composed, and bound by The Haddon Craftsmen, Inc.
Printed by The Murray Printing Company
HARPER & ROW, PUBLISHERS, INCORPORATED